FAITH IT FORWARD

FINDING FAITH AND ADVENTURE IN A WORLD OF FEAR AND HOPE DEFERRED

MEGAN PRENTICE

Because life has its challenges and joys, we need relationships with others along the way, especially with the Lord, our most important relationship of all. I have learned I don't just want the Lord; I need Him. I know some people can be intimidated by pursuing a relationship with the God of the Universe or may not know where to start. This book is dedicated to everyone genuinely seeking to know God and to do day-to-day relationship with Him. He is my life's greatest adventure. He can be yours, too.

CONTENTS

INTRODUCTION
THE GREATEST JOURNEY

It was a time when faith was entirely childlike and new. Not to say my faith isn't childlike anymore, but these were the days of "firsts" and fresh belief that anything could happen, because *it did*.

In those days, the words in the Bible seemed to pop off the page and play out before me as I walked through similar circumstances of the very words I read. I lived those words. It was the only way I was able to retain Scripture—by walking through it.

Since then, I've experienced the highs and lows of life. But I wouldn't have experienced life any other way. I would give anything to walk through it again and again—to know Jesus through it all because being with Him is where the joy erupted. The mountains and valleys were where the breakthrough and peace and deep, deep love for others came—where I felt the tender moments of being held by the Savior of the Universe.

No one has ever walked through it all with me like Jesus. I'm reminded of that fact as I write this, while listening to "No One Ever Cared For Me Like Jesus," just released by Steffany Gretzinger. I want you to feel the caring love of Jesus as you walk through my story. I want you to experience laughter and tears. And throughout these short stories, I will share some songs and scriptures that got me through. I encourage you to stop and listen as you read and journey with me, looking to Him to speak to your heart. I also challenge you to lean into surrender. Learning to let go and rest when I'm prone to "drive and strive" has been one of the greatest gems I've received in my faith journey.

After yet another season of surrender, Jesus brought me across the ocean to Hawaii while the world was on pause during COVID-19. I was handed a speeding ticket and offered absolutely no mercy my first week on the island. As I stared down at the yellow parchment, I felt God nudge me saying, "Slow down, Megan. There's a lot to be learned in the slow lane." Learning to be inconvenienced and to strip everything away (even mental distractions like killing bugs in my jungle bungalow) to strive to enter rest has brought me more fruit than I ever imagined.

The more we know Him, the more we discover ourselves. And all He asks us for is faith. Faith is a gift. And I felt an invitation from the Lord to not only focus on the great stories because they are not the complete reality. Life isn't one great experience after another. No, there are hard times, difficult days, but doing them all *with Him* is worthwhile. He makes things beautiful. He has made *me* beautiful. I have found something better than fleeting mountaintop experiences. I have met a loyal Friend who not only walks next to me through life's journey, but turns the heartache into fairytale endings, as long as I remain by His side.

"They" say that you can identify a counterfeit dollar by studying the real thing. That's what I do with Jesus. I keep my focus on the "real" thing, on Him, because counterfeits in life will take me off course. I'm inviting you to do the same—to keep Jesus as your focus. You will see yourself change before your very eyes, too. Maybe not right away, but you *will* have moments where you almost have to pinch yourself as an onlooker to your own life. In situations where you may have responded in fear, anger, or frustration in the past, you will find yourself responding from a place of wholeness, peace, patience, or joy. Transformation is unlike anything I've ever experienced because at its core is Jesus. It's remarkable.

I couldn't be more thankful for a friend, counselor, business partner, and comforter, all in one Person. He is steadfast and makes me feel "sane." I think every other onlooker and friend might have tossed in the towel (and some have) a while ago. But the Lord is really, truly, always, and forever *there*. He is there for me. He is there for you. If we keep our gaze on Him and allow Him to speak into our lives, we will see our "ugly" transform into beauty.

I am an entirely different person than I was over ten years ago when I met the Lord through an intense dream. My transformation hasn't been easy, but it's been worth every pain and hardship. I let Him change me because I *trust* the beauty that He produces. He's given me the ability to do so because He's proven Himself to me. Not just once. Not just twice. But over and over again. And you will see the same—it's a promise. He isn't partial to one person over another. He has the exact same love and desire for you that He does for me. He is simply looking for your *yes*. *Yes* to change. *Yes* to Him. *Yes* to the adventure and the tough times. *Yes* to the best faith stories. *Yes* to continuing to come back to Him, even when it doesn't make sense, and to truly living as your best self in a life of freedom.

Join me as we relive my faith adventures through the tippy-top mountain highs, deep longings in the waiting, and heartbreak valley lows to discover how real and all-encompassing the character of our Father and Friend in Heaven is—to see what a fun Adventure Partner He can be and what a beautiful Crying Shoulder He remains. He is closer and more relatable than any other person in this world. It's an honor to get to call Him a friend, and I am humbled by His constant acts of love. Let's journey together as I unravel my favorite character traits of my Closest Companion.

TRAIT I

MY ADVENTUROUS
TRAVEL BUDDY

CHAPTER 1

ENCOUNTERING GOD

*I*t all started in 2009. I was a college partier on the weekends, Thursday through Saturday, since naturally every University of Colorado student knew the weekend started early. During the week, I was a diligent student, and I attended church once a week with a friend—something I had only recently started to do. The messages at church spoke to me, so I figured why not. At that point in my life, it was all about me anyway. School was everything to me then, and success was life. Failing wasn't even in the Prentice vocabulary.

One weekend, I needed to retreat from the party scene to study. My parents' place was always a great respite, only a 45-minute drive from campus. Tired from all the partying and the "go-go-go" of life in Boulder, I plopped myself on their couch and vegged in between study sessions. It was an ordinary weekend, like any other. Sunday morning rolled around, and my parents dressed up for their church service in the suburbs, as they had done every Sunday for the past twenty years of my life. I could hear my Dad's footsteps approaching my bedroom that was still considered mine even though I was away to college. Slight dread filled my heart in anticipation of the presumed question, "Want to go to church?"

That was an easy, "No, I'm tired and have a lot of studying to do." Growing up, church was a boring pastime that felt very hypocritical and fake. I saw it as a huge waste of time for my efficient self, who could be either sleeping or studying instead.

My parents left, and I fell back into a deep sleep. What I was about to experience was unlike anything I had ever experienced before. My deep slumber turned into a dream, which became the room. No, not even the room. It became the world, but even more real than the world, if that's possible. I couldn't breathe. It felt dark, scary, and oppressive. I felt as if an elephant were stepping on my chest and wouldn't relent as I saw the scene of a genocide play out before me. I'm talking "Hotel Rwanda" style. Blood spilled out like a river and turned into an actual river as I saw African babies being murdered and tossed into the water. It. Was. Horrifying! It was like those scary virtual reality encounters at Disney World, but worse. Remember *Alien Encounter* where the alien broke out of the glass and breathed on your neck? It was that "real." I was up close and personal with the 3-D scene right in front of me.

And just like that, a tidal wave of ocean water came to the rescue and washed all the blood away. All heaviness lifted. Inexpressible peace fell like a thick blanket on the room as a huge wave crashed in. It reminded me of the tremendous waves surfed at Pipeline in Oahu. Inside the wave, I saw cursive script that read, "The Lord giveth what the Lord taketh away."

Immediately after, a determined male whisper, "Megan!" jolted me awake. It was kind of like when you hear a car alarm go off in the early morning, and it instantly sends your heart into a flutter. I knew it was God. His voice was expressive and authoritative. In that moment, I understood for the first time what "fear of the Lord" meant. It made me want to get low and hide under the bed. The grandness and weight were too much for my frail human body to bear, and He wasn't even sharing a millionth of what He carries on a daily basis. What I did know in that moment was God was real, and He wanted *me* to know it.

I typically don't dream. Or, I should say, I rarely remember if I do. I find dreams so fascinating, but during the time of this encounter, I found the Bible not so fascinating. I only read the Bible when I was required to many years before in Sunday school, and even though I grew up going to a church, I only knew one scripture. It was the one I had to memorize at church camp in order to take a ride on the zipline (a great way to get kids on the memorization train, if you ask me!). I guess I blocked out everything else. And even if I did read about Job in Sunday school (which I highly doubt was a topic of choice for first graders), I sure didn't know the story until delving in after this wild encounter.

"The Lord giveth *and* the Lord taketh away" was what I knew the Bible stated. Yet, the Lord spoke to me in a new and different way through the cursive script that scrolled across the tidal wave like subtitles at the end of a movie, "The Lord giveth *what* the Lord taketh away." It was a message *to me*. Little did I know then, it was God's promise I would get to stand on when the losses of life transpired. I got to see a short trailer of His grandness in the midst of the horror, pain, and loss in the world. And though the scene could have crushed me, there was a strange calming sense that came over me, knowing He had it all under His control. It's almost as if He was sharing a message that would get me through the many years to come. He cares enough to spur us on like that.

After that weekend, I returned to college, and life progressed as usual. I continued in my countless hours of studying and fell back into the party scene at my school. I mustered up the courage a couple of months after having the dream to ask my campus pastor for an interpretation of what it all meant. He was the pastor, so surely he should know, right? But he didn't. In fact, he made me feel a little crazy and as if what I had experienced wasn't real. I left my meeting with him just as confused as before, knowing what I had experienced was, *indeed*, the most real thing I had ever encountered. If he was the pastor and didn't have the answers, I wondered who did. (I'm not faulting him here. This was just my journey of navigating faith early on.)

Between tests and social life, I was a busy college gal. Yet, the desire for Africa seemed to loom in the background of my mind. I had already joined an anti-genocide group on campus prior to the dream, but I felt it was time to dedicate my all. Between Darfur awareness screenings and conferences, I decided to hit my knees and ask for an open door to Africa.

One day, while walking home from campus, I ran into a girl named Leah from my high school. She told me about this "thing" called "Musana," as if everyone knew what it was and I was the last to know. I played along and nodded my head until I heard her say, "Uganda." *That* was when I started to think, *Uganda . . . I know that's somewhere in Africa*, and the rest of what she had to say didn't matter to me. I just knew I needed to be involved.

Leah invited me over to her college home to tag necklaces for Musana. When I walked in, there were multicolored necklaces in several semi-organized piles. As I tip-toed around the piles, Leah explained how the Ugandan women and children from her organization hand-rolled the beads from paper and magazine clippings in order to raise money for their organization. Though popular now, back then it was a revolutionary concept! Countless necklaces later, I decided in my heart I was going to Africa with Musana, and there was nothing that could stop me.

Besides school, I cared about two things in life: Africa and running. Oh, wait. Actually, three things: Africa, running, and boys. I can't lie! While living only five blocks from the base of the majestic Flatirons, Boulder's iconic rock formations, I decided to train for a marathon. It was then or never, and being a bucket-list item, I decided to go for it.

When I broke the news to my parents, I imagine they probably rolled their eyes while smiling and shaking their heads at my goals. I don't blame them. I had not even run a half marathon! But, if I was going to do it, I was going to do it right. In our call, my mom mentioned an online schedule her friend raved about for her marathon training. The schedule looked better than my spontaneous runs, so I filled my calendar with the schedule and committed the next four and a half months to diligently following my new normal.

Somewhere toward the middle of my training, I heard someone mention how they were training for a cause. I figured, *Hey, if they can, so can I! I guess I will start today.* It was then that my marathon was no longer about me, but it became my motivation to get to Africa. No one knew my plan yet, not even my poor parents.

At some point, I decided to tell my parents I wanted to go to Africa. They laughed and said, "Yeah, right . . . in your dreams." Little did they know how right they were. Africa was in my dreams, and I was set on getting there somehow. I seemed to have always been a bit different than my parents. They always had it "together" and were much more planned in their decision-making. I have tended to follow the dreams in my heart, and as a former colleague put it, I made a way by "flying by the seat of my pants." Looking back, I honor my parents for being the stable ones while I grew into my wild and crazy dreams. I respect their caution and rules, but at the time, I wanted nothing more than to get to Africa. When I knew I wouldn't get their blessing on my dream to travel to Africa, I knew I had to take matters into my own hands. Not having my parents' blessing wasn't the best way to go about things, but "when you know, you know," and you have to chase the dream.

As an "all in" kind of a gal, the next time I went home, I snagged the family address book with all my parents' friends' addresses in it. I typed and signed about thirty letters describing my endeavors to run a marathon to raise funds toward my trip to Africa. As I licked the seals shut, I figured I should probably tell my parents what I was up to before mailing them out. While staring at the large stack of envelopes, my nerves spiked as I made the call. Again, maybe not the best strategy to honor my parents, but I was young and selfish at the time. They were mad. Rightfully so, but they ultimately came around to the idea since they knew their daughter was bull-headed and they weren't going to win this one.

And so, the Africa goal became a plan. On October 18, 2009, I ran my first marathon in under four hours, which was followed by a tight calf muscle, inhaling two burritos scarfed down back-to-back, and a four-hour nap in the same room where I had *the dream*.

Later that week, sponsorship letters were returned with checks amounting to a little over $700. That combined with a little income from my side job gave me the $2,500 I needed to fly to Uganda for the summer of 2010. This was one of many adventures, but my grandest ones were yet to come.

CHAPTER 2

BUILDING HISTORY IN THE PASSENGER'S SEAT

$\mathcal{I}$'ve always been a "solo rider." I absolutely love people, and I have many incredible friends, but travel runs deep in my veins. I wouldn't make it in this life without my community and their powerhouse prayers. Yet, there's something about being able to pick up and leave on random adventures whenever I want. Hawaii for the weekend? Sure! Australia during a tough break up? Why not? That's why once I met Jesus and saw the way He operates, I knew I met my match in an adventure buddy, and I decided not only to invite Him along, but to give Him the driver's seat for our nail-biting adventures.

I have a lot of favorite plane stories, but the best ones are the ones that kept me on the edge of my seat, literally. I have to admit I gained incredible favor from the Lord when my mom decided to work for an airline. The airline provided free flight benefits for life to her, my dad, and her soon-to-be children. Have you ever experienced favor? It's getting something you don't earn or deserve for absolutely no reason other than the fact that God loves you. That's what this was. Before I was even a thought in my mom's mind, God already knew me and decided He was going to give His adventurous daughter (that's me!) free flights to meet Him in the most intimate ways as we traveled the world together. God tends to do that. He is outside of time and likes to offend our minds with how much He really cares. He meets us in our most intimate desires and even in the mundane day-to-day. I've seen it so many times, and I'm taking you along for the ride so you can start to see Him in your life, too!

I can't remember the first time I got the last seat on the plane while flying standby because it became a common pattern with the Lord, but I do remember being more excited than ever to get to the airport every time I traveled. Unlike many others who look at the airport as a stress-packed, heart attack-inducing rat race, it was my happy place—my Disney World—and even the lines were part of the fun. I knew Jesus and I would get to tell jokes with the TSA, we'd get to pray over people in line (without them knowing it—kind of like covert spies trying to love-bomb the airport).

Best of all, I'd get to curl up on an airport seat with Him while telling Him the deepest desires of my heart or a funny story that happened that week. He was my Best Friend. Still is. But back then, it was like the honeymoon phase of our relationship. I loved dates with Jesus in the airport, sharing my heart and feeling His love envelope me while watching planes take off and seeing people run with luggage from place to place. But that's the funny thing. I was so caught up in Him I hardly noticed the havoc going on around me. I guess that's what happens when you're in love.

In navigating my newfound relationship with God, I didn't have context for what "friendship" with the Lord meant, yet I was living it anyway. And this was the first phase in my life where I slowed down enough to see His love-actions toward me as He

Building History in the Passenger's Seat | 11

repeatedly proved His love in tangible ways I could recognize. There is a sense of security in love that we all crave when we know the other person is "all in" and there's no doubt they will ever leave. It gives us a freedom to be ourselves, totally and completely ourselves. I knew I had found that kind of special love. I felt "like a million bucks" as I floated down airport concourses, cracking jokes with Jesus and being my goofy self. I felt accepted. I felt free. I had found the greatest kind of romance that people search for their entire lives. I never wanted Him to leave. The beautiful thing is He never will.

CHAPTER 3

MAUI IN PARADISE

J decided to be bold and push my luck with my first solo trip to Maui as a young twenty-something. I was meeting a friend who I had gone to business school with at the University of Colorado. Though I used to travel to Hawaii nearly every year with my family, there was something exhilarating about navigating the world without the ones who raised me. The independence and the adventure that Jesus brings were already the most incredible combination. At this point, my faith had grown massively during my airport adventures with the Lord because of my personal "plane favor." Up until that point in time, I had gotten on every flight (at least ten or so). In the standby world, that's a miracle in itself! I decided to test the limits with my connecting flight in LAX and sign up for an "illegal connection," meaning I only had ten minutes once my flight landed to get to the next gate before the doors closed. Why? Well, because, why not? When you're royalty and have been treated as such, you can start to get bold. The reality is we are all sons and daughters of the Lord; we just have to step into believing it.

The Los Angeles airport can be a bit of a game of chess in hopping over people, airport carts, and conveyor belts to make connecting flights. Unfortunately, my flight from Denver was delayed ten minutes, so once I was in a confirmed seat, I knew it was time to start praying. I think I prayed the whole flight to Los Angeles. In between prayers and prior to landing, I used an app to find my next departure gate (thank goodness for in-flight WIFI), and it just so happened to be the gate *directly* across from my arrival gate. Coincidence? I think not. That was my first little wink from Jesus.

And so, the riveting race began. It almost felt like an intense scavenger hunt trying to get to the next clue, but on a grand scale with planes and people who weren't aware of the game. The flight attendant announced our arrival as we touched down, and I looked at the time. My next flight was due to shut its doors any minute. I could feel the excitement racing through my veins as I grabbed my carry-on bag and dashed to the neighboring gate to get my seat for the next flight. I had a knowing ahead of time, in my very being, that the flight would still be there *and* the Lord had a seat with my name on it.

And He did. Yet again. In a matter of two minutes from when the doors opened on plane number one, I ran to the counter, caught some smiles and jokes from the gate agents as they printed my ticket and rolled their eyes (kindly), and then sat down in the designated seat the Lord had for His adrenaline-junkie daughter on the second flight. I was on my way to Hawaii.

Even after the eight-hour journey across the ocean, my heart was dancing with excitement as I landed in the warmth of Maui. Carry-on bag in hand, I walked straight to passenger pick-up where my friend, local to Maui, greeted me with a beautiful handmade lei and her rickety black truck. Her cute little truck was so low to the ground that I was sure all four tires were flat. With a closer look, it turned out they were not. As I threw my bag in the truck bed, the truck seemed to sink a little lower, if that was possible, and we were on our way. I love local experiences, and to this day, that black truck still fills me with joy.

Our first stop was the grocery store for drinks, fresh poke, seaweed, and rice. Next stop, the white sandy beach. As we arrived and parked at the beach, I noticed we were the only ones there! Everyone else must have been getting checked into hotels. Somehow, I won the lottery with great friends and VIP front row seats to a make-your-own-sushi lunch on the secluded beach. I kicked off my flip-flops (known as slippers in Hawaii), popped the hand-rolled sushi in my mouth, and dove right into the ocean, only 45 minutes after landing. What a dream!

I was basking in the Lord's continued favor as I floated in the warm, salty water, staring out into the endless blue. The mixture of the saltwater and sun felt like the equivalent of ten visits to the spa. I could have basked all day out there, until I saw the waters disrupted by a large animal swimming directly at me, "full speed ahead." My heart skipped some beats. At least two. I sighed after realizing it was only a sea turtle and not a pointy-finned shark. The fear of getting mauled in the ocean lifted as I breathed in the salty air and mustered up, "Sea turtle!" My friend laughed and yelled back that being within a couple feet of a sea turtle was a rarity and very special. Isn't it funny how fear in the present moment can turn into some of our greatest memories? When you're with your Favorite Travel Buddy, whether in the busiest airports or the warm Pacific Ocean, every instant feels like heaven.

CHAPTER 4

UGANDA BE KIDDING ME

"This is Africa" was a common phrase used among volunteers that I first heard when our private taxi broke down on the way to Musana. My friend's organization was four hours outside the main city of Kampala in Uganda. It was the summer of 2010, and I was just starting Musana's five-week volunteer program. After an hour's wait while trying to decipher even one word of Lugandan, I was sure we had to be on our way to some kind of motor vehicle shop. But no. They had a better plan because this was Africa.

Standing outside our stranded sedan, I stared into the thick jungle, hoping to see some monkeys and pretending not to look nervous when a "boda" motorcycle arrived with a brand-new timing belt. Apparently in Uganda, they bring the shop to you! Our roadside mechanic fixed it right then and there on the one-lane highway with cars flying by at max speed. I continued to stare out into the lush forest and tried to get used to the fumes of burning trash that would hit my nostrils every so often.

Besides falling in love with the kids, playing intense "football" in a field of cows, and snuggling up to my first hippo on the opposite side of my tent while on safari, nothing out of the ordinary happened during my first trip to Uganda. What did happen was I totally and completely fell in love with the people and simple lifestyle. I knew I'd be going back.

And I was right. East Africa became a frequent trip over the ensuing years. From volunteering with my friends' organizations to doing hospital assessments and "boots on the ground" trips for several nonprofits, Mozambique, Uganda, and Kenya almost became my second homes. Some trips were all expenses paid, and others were more "bootlegged." I enjoyed the adventure of five-star hotels with linen sheets only to find myself in a squatty potty with flies heading in the wrong direction three hours later.

To that point, I had experienced so many plane miracles through standby passes that my pride flared up into a state of entitlement. Each trip, I pushed the limits with getting to the airport "just in time" for boarding. I would pray silently, *knowing* I would get on, and not give into worry. Yet, I seemed to step out of the realm of faith and right into entitlement. Thankfully, the Lord is kind, generous, and gracious and loves to come alongside us and correct us when we need a shift in mindset or behavior. He showed me what "His mercies are new every morning" meant and what "grace" looked like as I learned to meander the bowling alley of faith by hitting the gutters every now and again. He's a good dad. That's what dads do. They help their kiddos learn, and when children get a little out of line, they give us a little "tap-tap-taparoo" in the right direction.

This story is fun. It shows my pride, humbled by a mixture of His grace, spunk, and faithfulness all wrapped up together with a pretty bow on top to show it was definitely His hand at work.

After three years of working at the medical nonprofit I grew to love and then not love toward the end, I decided it was long past my time to go. Through prayer and with the Lord of the Universe on my side, I took the biggest leap of faith yet. I left "stability" to pursue my dream of launching sustainable businesses in Africa with the goal of funding nonprofits in surrounding communities. It seemed like a quality dream to me, and nothing stood in my way, so I resigned.

At that same time, I felt the Lord nudging me to head back to Uganda for a visionary trip. A newer group of friends just so happened to be planning a trip out to another organization called ROWAN (check them out: loverowan.org), only about twenty minutes from Musana where I first left part of my heart. As I tend to do, I started dreaming up business ideas and ways to make a living in a foreign land. I had what I thought was a spectacular idea to move out to Uganda as a consultant for nonprofits, to be their "point person" for any "boots on the ground" tasks. It turns out nonprofits don't have a lot of extra income to hire in-country staff, so I proposed the idea of working for multiple organizations I had connected with over the years. When that plan was set in my mind, I knew I needed one last thing: money.

Looking back, I had the funds in the bank to get to Uganda, but my poverty mentality at the time led me to believe otherwise. Poverty mindsets are more detrimental than physical poverty because mindsets create reality; but that's another book for another time. Let's just say I would later have a lot less money in the bank after the loss of my business. It's all about perspective. Yet, as a young and frugal entrepreneur, I had it in my mind that I needed to find a donor.

Sometimes I ask God to make decisions evident by providing one way or another. This time, I requested financial provision as a sign I was to fly halfway across the world. I prayed and prayed and prayed some more for the finances to come through. Via email, I asked two gracious donors from the nonprofit for the $3,000 I needed for airfare and in-country costs. One came back with a hard *no*. The other gave me radio silence for what felt like forever.

One long week after sending the emails, I got a call from my Bible study leader, and I let her in on my vision to fly to Uganda in less than two weeks, though I had yet to receive any funding. She responded with, "Let's pray."

I'm a "doer," and I loved her boldness because, as I had already experienced so many times before, prayer gets things in motion. When we said, "Amen" (which means "let it be"), I opened my email. I can't remember if I dropped the phone or cried, but I know I was in complete awe of God's perfect timing. It was my first time experiencing what the Bible says about God knowing what we need before we ask Him (see Matt. 6:8). I'm talking milliseconds before asking.

I wonder if I still have access to that email. Either way, not even a full second before the Amen, I got an email from the second donor saying he couldn't provide the $3,000, but he could provide $1,000 toward my dream. (If you are reading this, thank you. You know who you are.) I was ecstatic! I said a quick "thanks" and "bye" to my leader and busted out the calculator while searching flights from Brussels to Entebbe, Uganda. I knew if I could fly standby to Brussels, hopefully the $1,000 could cover the rest of the trip.

The flight from Brussels to Uganda was $660. I immediately called my friend Kelsey, co-founder of ROWAN, and she said she could discount the trip to a bare minimum of $300 just to cover costs of food and gas. I looked up flights on the intranet of my standby airline, and the costs of the taxes came to $43. Guess the total? $1,003. Ha! I told Jesus that I supposed I could pay $3 for the trip (since, after all, I did have money, though I thought I didn't). It's cool how the Lord meets us where we are, poverty mindset and all.

I called Kelsey back and confirmed I would be on that plane with the group, heading to Uganda in less than two weeks. Oh, and guess which airline the team just so happened to be on? Mine (which wasn't a traditional airline to take to Brussels). If you aren't convinced of God's faithfulness beyond coincidence, lean in. It gets better!

We got to the airport in the wee hours, but we were all "bright-eyed and bushy-tailed," looking forward to the adventure ahead. We arrived at the gate, and by this time, everyone on the team knew of my wild plane adventures with Jesus, probably two times over. I *had to* brag on God's faithfulness time and again. It was too much to contain! I told them nonchalantly I would get on the plane "no problem." The Lord had gotten me that far. As they all got up to board, I started to have a thought: *Maybe I should at least check the board and see what number I am on the standby list.*

They all boarded, and I was still confident I'd be seeing them in minutes—until I looked at the screen. It said they were now overbooked, a major shift from being open the day before. I was number two on the standby list to get to Newark, and I had a paid ticket for the third leg of my trip from Brussels to Uganda. I *had* to make this plane. It wasn't looking good, especially as I was flying in faith on someone else's dollars. I started to sweat and asked the Lord to please reserve me a seat. I felt an invitation to kneel on the airport ground and pray. As I did, my heart shifted from entitlement to humility. A few long stares from the gate agent assisted in humbling me. Nonetheless, I kept my focus on the Lord and prayed, "Jesus, please, please, please get me on this plane. You've brought me this far. Forgive me for being entitled instead of faith-filled. I know there is a difference. Please give me favor with this gate agent. And please open up just one spot for me on this plane." I sent out an SOS prayer text to my friends who were already cozied up on the plane. I could tell through their worried texts they were getting nervous, too. I heard the agent announce a name—and it wasn't mine.

After eleven minutes (which felt more like thirty) of kneeling and praying on the airport ground with the gate agent glaring my way, my numb legs began to tingle as I nervously pondered what could possibly be the delay. I prayed yet again, more for comfort than anything else. Then it happened. I got a familiar warmhearted feeling in my chest that accompanied a "Megan Prentice" over the speaker as the gate agent printed my ticket! I gasped, sighed in relief, and thanked Jesus, all at the same time. The agent walked me and the ticket over to scan me onto the plane.

I was on my way to Uganda! It didn't come without discomfort, though. Usually, the gate agents give you the ticket, and you're home-free to board. This agent was like a fire-breathing dragon who, for whatever reason, followed close behind and escorted me down the long corridor, across the bridge, and into my fairytale vessel. The whole time, I was thanking Jesus and dancing inside, amid the resentment I felt emanating off him. I'm not sure if his presence, my desperate prayers, or the large backpack I was carrying caused the sweating bullets under my arms, but the pool of water grew as he opened the overhead bins. There was space (barely) for one more bag. He, and the rest of the plane that had been boarded for fifteen minutes now, stared without blinking as I shimmied off my backpack and tried to shove my overfilled bag into the last little space. Still wide-eyed, and now drenched, everyone watched as I detached each little ribbon to remove the top of my backpack in order to maneuver the bag into its temporary home. I felt like I was entertaining at the circus but for the most unpopular act. The crowd was not amused. I didn't care. I got it in, and I was on my way to Newark, en route to Uganda!

Jesus knows my heart for adventure, and He sure likes to keep me reeling for more. If I've learned anything about my Co-pilot, it's that He doesn't like to leave room for questioning or coincidence. So, to be sure He gets the glory, He might make us sweat a little to be sure we know He's still Head Captain. When our hearts are tuned to see what He will do next, that's where the glory happens. He will give us the last seat on the exact plane as our friends, and as a little wink, He might leave *just* enough room for our bags to fit in the overhead bin.

CHAPTER 5

MIRACULOUS AIRPORT CARTS

And then there was Guatemala in 2014. That one was truly a miraculous trip. My friend Jenny, living the dream in Los Angeles, and I, still in my hometown city of Denver, decided to flee the winter cold for an exciting adventure. The only stipulations were that it had to be exotic, foreign, and tropical. We wanted to go "third world," but we only had a week of vacation time and not a lot of money. Neither of us had been to Central or South America, and I had a co-worker who raved about Antigua and Lake Atitlán in Guatemala. One of the perks of working with an international nonprofit was having colleagues who doubled as travel agents. Jenny and I made loose outlines of hostels and hotels and left the rest up to chance. She bought her ticket, and I investigated standby flights.

Being the "experienced" international traveler of our duo, I wanted to beat Jenny to Guatemala since it was her first big getaway. I figured I would fly in a day earlier to test out the hostel pillows and community ping-pong table. Flights looked good—until that morning. I made it to Houston, no problem. It was the flight to Guatemala City that was the nail-biter, at least for my parents. They called an hour into my layover in Houston and said in a not-so-promising tone, "What's your backup plan, Megan? You're not going to get on this plane." Knowing the flights the whole next day and a few days after were over-booked, this was it. This one flight was my only chance to get to Guatemala.

As with my other plane experiences, I can honestly say, up until that point, I had not even looked at the number of seats filled or standbys on the list *because* I had experienced God's provision so many times before. Plane favor, that's what I call it. It's real, and I was banking on it again. So much so, I didn't have the slightest doubt in my mind I would get on this plane. I just *knew* I'd get on.

Have you ever gone into a situation knowing something would happen before it does—mostly because it did every single time leading up to that point? It's called history, baby. People say that history repeats itself, but even more, creating history with someone else is what forms the bond of trust that leads to a no-doubt, deeply rooted, solid foundation.

In my plane adventures with the Lord, that's exactly what we were doing: creating history together. We created an unshake-able trust. He loves to lavish us over and over until we find ourselves in such a place of blind faith that we don't even check the screens or plane capacities anymore. We simply show up to full flights with a large bin of popcorn and say, "Make miracles happen, Lord," as we stare starry-eyed at our Dad's heroic works. That's the easiest way to walk out faith. Just step out, ask Him to show up, and watch Him work wonders. When you see Him follow through, it will increase your faith for the next time. And when He shows up again (which He will), your faith increases even more, and you've now created history with the God of the Universe. It's amazing, really. He's not a genie. He's just a very good Dad who is always there for His kids. And He loves when we make time for Him throughout our day. He loves when we prioritize conversations with Him over anyone else. When we have hearts purely for Him, He reveals more of Himself to us. That's a *real* relationship.

I must admit I felt fear creep into my heart when my parents brought me back to the screen stating the facts. I was number eleven on the standby list, and there were only seven seats available on the plane. In the faith game, facts and numbers don't run God. He runs them. He doesn't show up to scenarios that make sense. He likes to shatter our concept of "should be's" and create something out of nothing.

When I snapped back to reality and my remembrance of how the Lord had saved me the last seat three different times before this, I started to re-partner with faith. God gave me the *last* seat! *Three different trips in a row!* I'm not talking one-hour flights either. One experience was that first leg of my trip to Uganda! That doesn't *just happen*. I'd say, personally, that anything beyond "two" qualifies for a miracle rather than coincidence. He sure does like to keep us on the edge of our seats though, doesn't He? And because God likes to make Himself known, most times He makes us sweat a little. I believe it's to glorify Himself so we can't take any credit. It's more fun that way. Math in the Kingdom of God is more fun, too. *Faith plus action equals favor.* And favor supersedes the natural world we live in.

"Last call for Boarding Group 5." I hung up the phone with my parents and their not-so-hopeful thoughts of me getting on the plane. In a moment, I recalled my most recent flight experiences with the Lord, and my chest slowly and strongly began to flood with the same familiar warming sensation I had in the past, the one telling me, "You're getting on this plane." That's how He talks to me. In feelings. In repetition. In numbers, sometimes. But, this time, it was a feeling of warmth, the same way He had spoken the last three times I ended up getting on the plane.

"Oh, my gosh! I cannot *wait* to see how You show up, Lord!" I was so excited to see how He was going to pull this one off because it seemed nearly impossible. The other standbys boarded, and there were five seats left.

I felt a strong impression to get down on my knees and pray in the middle of the airport. Slightly embarrassed, but knowing God speaks crazy things, like the time Jesus spit in mud to heal a blind man's eyes, I decided I'd rather be obedient and embarrassed than disobedient and regretful. I got down on my knees in the middle of the airport gate, which was now empty except for the hopeful standby passengers eagerly waiting for any open seats. A family of five was called to the counter to claim the last of the five seats. As I kneeled, I was confused, but still knew with everything in me that I would get on that plane because I had gotten confirmation from God Himself.

Out of nowhere, an airport cart came speeding up, stopping abruptly in front of our gate. Within a minute, a man in his early thirties sprinted from the cart to the plane as the gate agents were making their last announcements before shutting the doors. Because the last-minute traveler made the flight, the family of five decided to stay behind and wait to fly together on the next flight. That left four seats open. The gate agents called one name. And then another. And another. Then I heard, "Megan Prentice." My heart leapt with excitement as they scanned my ticket and scooted me into my seat while closing the cabin doors.

It was a whirlwind. It was the biggest "high" I'd experienced yet. My friends, though, might tell you I say that every time. I was on "Cloud 9" the whole way to Guatemala. Though it wasn't my first "last seat" standby experience, I still got the same exhilarating rush in my stomach because Jesus has a way of keeping me reeling for more in His never-ending surprise adventures.

Life with the Lord never gets old. And even though He doesn't meet me with the same faith-building adventure of "last seat" plane rides these days, He invites me into even more excitement in new and different ways. He's ever creating, ever adventurous, ever fun, ever romantic, and ever trustworthy. I think those are the best kinds of friends. Well, there's actually no friend who can compare to all that He is. I'm just thankful I get to "strap-up" as co-pilot next to the all-time Best Adventure Buddy. He even outdoes Himself every time.

*Jumping for joy with my friend Jenny on our mini
hike overlooking the city of Antigua, Guatemala,
as a volcano erupted in the distance.*

TRAIT II

INTENTIONAL INTERIOR DECORATOR

CHAPTER 6

TRASH INTO TREASURE

*I*t's not every day you get to decorate your bedroom with the Lord of the Universe. Doesn't that *sound* cool? I bet you're imagining elaborate walls lined in gold and bowls filled with incense (if you grew up in the church, anyway). But my experience in decorating with Jesus has been a bit different and, quite honestly, a whole new kind of fun than my travel adventures.

I thought my heart was the most alive through travel. It turns out there were parts of my heart I didn't even know could be awakened until the Lord showed them to me. I had no idea how much I longed to create a space of freedom, peace, and joy to share with others until the moment presented itself. That's what's fun about the Lord. He helps us unwrap the gifts and beauty within us on this wild road called life. I believe that's *how* we end up feeling fully alive because He really does know us better than we know ourselves, and He wants to help us discover the gold He has put inside us.

A few years ago, while owning a faith-based fitness studio, I decided to take yet another leap of faith and move out of my parents' house. Moving out meant leaving stability for a spontaneous, always shifting, always chaotic in the best way possible home with four other Christian women. Community living. Have you ever done it? I never thought I would enter this lifestyle again after college, but apparently, I needed it because the Lord put a strange desire in my heart to live with several Christian women. I say strange because it was foreign to how I lived in the past, living selfishly and very much alone. Don't get me wrong. I have always loved people, but I also valued being able to choose when to interact with them. I liked doing it on my time, in my way. That's not even a concept in community living. It's all people, all the time, and most often, when it's least convenient.

I grew to love the new lifestyle, despite the endless dishes piled high in the kitchen sink. There's something beautiful about always coming home to someone you can process your day with, cook with, laugh with, or even cry with. We entered the home with intentionality. We pushed one another to pursue our dreams, and we navigated relationships, some of which turned into marriages. The season was a gift, and I always tell people it helped shape who I am today.

The one caveat when we all moved into our new home together: Everyone wanted the upstairs bedrooms. Two girls had to share a room, and that's where I put my foot down. Being the oldest in the house, I needed my own space, and I was more than willing to pay the difference for it. After the wrestle of conversations about rooms, I knew the Lord was telling me to surrender and to take the downstairs bedroom. It wasn't much of a site at all; in fact, it was technically supposed to be an office. It had an average of three outlets on each wall, no closet, and two small windows that I'm not sure my hips would fit through if the house did go up in flames. But, if the Lord was nudging, I knew it was the right choice.

Growing up, I never cared to decorate or make a space my own. I always admired ambiance, but I came to the conclusion it just wasn't for me to be the brains behind the operation. Not to mention, decorating seemed like a lot of effort, and in our home, budgeting had the upper hand (thanks, Dad, for teaching us your phenomenal budgeting abilities)! It wasn't until I moved into the "Queens" home, as we called ourselves, that I started to truly dream with Jesus about my favorite shelving, colors, and furniture. My room was my secret place with Him, and whether I spent my time with Him there or not, I knew He cared about the details, not just a little bit, but a lot. I didn't know how much until the next month of renovations unfolded.

I settled into my new room after painting the walls a simple hand-me-down tan color from my parents' house. (Note to those wanting to make a new space "home": paint! It helps give you ownership and that "new" feeling.) In the dreaming process, I hardly maneuvered my queen mattress down the narrow staircase before the blueprint for my new room was complete. I had every square inch mapped out on my new favorite app full of decorators around the world. Though it's not something I could add to my resume, I had become a Pinterest connoisseur.

I pinned everything that brought my heart to life: a mirror atop a crate to fill the dark corner, a world map to remind me of my travels, a headboard made of fencing, and a wooden bedside table that nearly touched the ceiling. Later, my boyfriend informed me the bedside table I was drooling over was actually an old wooden ladder with small slabs of wood running perpendicular to the steps to make neat-looking shelves. He continued to say, "But that will be difficult to find, and if you do find it, the ladder will probably be a pricey antique." That's not quite what my frugal ears wanted to hear.

So, I resorted to prayer and asked Jesus for His decorating help.

If you know me well, you know that, when I commit to something, I do it, and you'd better get out of the way. It's part of my personality, and most likely one of the reasons the Lord has had to pull me back from the collar to tell me to stop and smell the roses along the journey. I like to get things done. "It's how You wired me, Lord," I've reminded Him often.

About a month into moving, I decided it had to be *that day* to get my decor in order, or it wouldn't happen. I could no longer stare at the blank, tan walls and nothingness surrounding my queen bed. My boyfriend decided to help, and we made it into a little date day, which turned into a date night and continued into the wee hours of the morning. We sanded and painted and sanded some more to give my childhood furniture an updated "Shabby Chic" look. We even browsed Craigslist and found free fencing for my headboard. The fencing called to us from a nearby alleyway, so we hopped in the car for a field trip and much-needed break.

After returning home and digging out my poor Honda from the masses of wood, I watched as my boyfriend transformed the fencing into a beautiful headboard. My vision was nearly complete, with the exception of a few more wooden panels for the base of the headboard, the bedside table, wooden jewelry hangers, and a handmade hanging shelf.

The next morning, astonished our dreamer-hearts couldn't outfit an entire room in one day, we dove in for round two of our carpentry skills. We returned yet again to the same alley and scavenged as many pieces as would fit in my little Honda Accord. As we drove off in a mad dash, ready to conquer the vision, my boyfriend stopped me about ten feet into our drive home and relayed, "Wait, hold on. Reverse! I think I saw a ladder, but it probably belonged to someone."

There, in that *exact* same alleyway in Englewood, Colorado, where I was gifted wood for the headboard, was an old, rickety, wooden ladder leaning up against the fence with a sign on it that read, "FREE."

That wooden ladder, with how specific a request it was and how strategically placed in a "random" alley, not listed on Craigslist in the middle of suburbia, but waiting for *me* to come and pick it up—that made my heart *gush*. There's nothing that makes me feel more seen. There's nothing that makes my heart feel more loved than knowing the God of the entire world cares so deeply about my decorating desires that He divinely orchestrated for someone to retire their old ladder.

I always like to guess the other side of the story. Was a painter leaving his life's work and never wanted to look at another ladder? Or did his wife urge him to get rid of the "eyesore" with splashes of multicolored paint everywhere? Either way, their trash became my treasure in perfect accordance with our 24-hour turnaround time for more wood. What are the odds? If only I had a dollar for every time I've said that about Jesus. . . .

To this day, that ladder is still my favorite gift from the Lord. I think mostly because my heart was so surprised. I didn't know God truly cared about "stuff" like that. I know He cares about me and having a relationship with me, but I guess I didn't know that meant decorating, too. Turns out it does. Oh, and by the way, we ended up completing the vision of the room with the jewelry hangers *and* the hanging shelf when my boyfriend surprised me with them as my birthday gifts later that month. The total sum of my entire interior decorating was $8, which is what I paid for a pillow cover to support an organization in

Kenya. More than I could ask or imagine, indeed—and on a budget, too!

CHAPTER 7

HAMMOCKING

*I*t was always my dream to move to the ocean. Door after door closed, and thirteen years after my first itch, I finally decided to try again, despite the upsets of the past. I pondered Australia, South Africa, and finally landed on Hawaii because I had friends already living on the Big Island. Community makes transition easier, so it was an easy *yes* when a space miraculously opened up for me in a little *ohana* (guest home) right next to my friends.

With beachy living, comes ocean-inspired decor! Did I want to go for a "beachy" ambiance? Or how about white, sleek, and minimalist? How about both? It sounds excessive, but envisioning the decor of my new ohana kept me up at night prior to my first big move. You would think it was the fear of the pandemic keeping me up, but no, I stayed up all hours of the night excitedly surfing the web for shaggy rugs, macramé pillows, a hanging hammock chair, and any other necessities to ship out to Kona, Hawaii.

I spent more than $8 this time around, but the Lord's surprises were far greater than our last interior decorating extravaganza. It felt like I went from a young woman to an adult home, the ones you see in the magazines or the "you should be here" places on social media. Yet, the gift didn't come without frustration, and I can honestly say I did not expect it in that time or place. Jesus tends to do that. When I want something right away, it doesn't come, yet when I am not expecting it, He blindsides me with the most overwhelmingly thoughtful gift. He's good at spoiling us and humbling us at the same time.

The worldwide pandemic and quarantine season became a time of family and creativity. Toward the beginning, I was living at my parents' house, and I didn't see a single friend for two and a half months straight, and I can honestly say I did not get tired of hanging out with my parents. It wasn't always the case, and that's another book for another time, but I really grew to love my parents as friends rather than parents. My mom and I would go on hour-and-a-half-long walks daily, and sometimes my dad would join. Our overly excited pup was always along for the adventure.

After walks, we dreamt up meals we used to drool over in restaurants in the days of old and then tag-teamed whipping up the chef's special for the night from the "what's left in the fridge" recipes and ingredients. If we didn't have it, we made our own whatever "it" was. And surprisingly, "it" was always good! We made everything from Thai chicken lettuce wraps to cashew-crusted mahi-mahi with pineapple salsa on top. Some days, I would go out and play tennis with Dad after filming some worshipful fitness routines and practicing guitar.

My move had now been delayed two and a half months. Though, as I have learned over time, what felt like delay to me, in God's eyes, was actually right on time. I walked through the full cycle of grief through frustration, anger, and surrender as I asked the Lord what He truly had for me in this unforeseen season. In an unexpected way, the delay brought healing and healthy creativity. It led me to surrender and honor my parents and their wishes during the unknown season. Our relationships grew, and I also stepped into my own kind of renaissance with the Lord.

One night, while in full-force decorating mode, a hammock chair and macramé were on my mind as I continued to peruse Pinterest and prepare to pack for Hawaii. My mom and I left at our usual time, around 3:30 in the afternoon to walk our dog. It must have been a Sunday because trash day is Monday, and as we were talking, I passed by our neighbor's recycle bin that had two items in it: a cardboard box and—wait for it—*a hammock!*

My heart started to race as I began to think of all the macramé patterns I would get to practice for free on this damaged outdoor hammock, especially as macramé pillows were trending online for over $70 a pop. There was no way I wanted to spend the same price on one pillow that I did for my recent area rug purchase. No cigar. This was an invitation to try out my crafty side during the slow pandemic months. I was hesitant in my abilities, yet so excited to explore this new side of me that I cut the walk short with Mom to circle back and grab the hammock. Our dog disapproved of my detour. He kept looking back at me, motioning with his nose to follow him. Even his cute proddings couldn't get me off track of my newfound project.

With the hammock in hand, I returned to my parents' place, only to discover nearly all the threads were still intact. Knowing I had nothing to lose since it was *free* material, I must have gotten a nudge from Jesus telling me to "go for it" because, before I knew it, I was tying a knot here and a knot there and hanging the new hammock chair from a branch to see what else needed to be doctored up. Chains were breaking. Yes, physically with the strong metal cutters to release unnecessary weight from the chain links on my new hanging chair, but also in the spiritual realm. Little did I know, with every knot I tied, I was breaking free from the lies I had told myself growing up. The ones that whispered, *You're not crafty,* and *You'll never be able to do it like them.*

By the time my mom returned, I had a brand-new hammock chair, but not just any hammock chair from Amazon. I'm talking a one-of-a-kind, Jesus-inspired, hammock chair with fringe on the side and metal rings large enough to put bamboo through the top once I arrived at my tropical paradise living room. My *exact* vision. And there's always a "cherry" on top in the Kingdom. I just so happened to have enough material left to make a large macramé wall hanging. Both became signature pieces displayed in my beachy bungalow. I didn't realize it at the time, but those pieces were the umph I needed to launch into my self-confidence journey of creativity.

Jesus surprised me with beachy furnishings while still in my dry home state of Colorado. The Lord is so complex. Not only was He sowing into my next season *before* I had even packed my bags, but He was also sowing into the greater treasure of believing in my own abilities to *create.* And not create ugly things like I had told myself for so long, but to create something *beautiful* that people actually admired, that *I* admired. After all, He is the Creator of all things, and we are made in His image to create like He does. The Lord could have easily given me a store-bought hammock chair and macramé wall hanging that day. But He didn't. He knew I had more inside me that needed to be discovered.

And the discovery continued, in the kitchen, through learning guitar, and even in writing this book. Little did I know at the time that by stepping into my hammock-making abilities, the Lord gave me the confidence I needed to keep believing in myself for the season to come. My creativity never came because I felt qualified. It came because my Papa in heaven showed me *I can*. He gave me the materials, and I just started tying the knots.

My long-awaited beachy bungalow in Hawaii centered around my one-of-a-kind hammock, and the sanctuary space where the majority of this book was written.

TRAIT III

DISTRIBUTOR OF THE WORLD'S LARGEST LOST & FOUND

CHAPTER 8

KEYS FROM THE KINGDOM

I tend to misplace things on a regular basis. The items I like to play hide-and-seek with most often are my keys. There was a season where I lost my keys so frequently that, if I didn't have Papa God and my earthly dad, I don't know how I would have survived daily life. During this "lost keys" chapter of life, I lived solo in a studio apartment in the outskirts of Denver just a mile from the football stadium. Though I'm not a raving football fan, I was thrilled when I scored free last-minute tickets to a sold-out Broncos' playoff game. We won the game, but the "high" didn't last long, as I discovered my keys had jumped out of my pocket sometime during the sold-out game with 77,000 people in attendance!

I had ideas of breaking into my garden-level studio, but to no avail, I landed at my parents' house, thankful to have a place to crash and one spare car key to get me around until my full set of keys were returned. It was a stressful time at work, and though I could have easily called a locksmith, it seemed more convenient to vacation at my parents' house (closer to my work) and *pray*. *Two full days* later, after a lot of faithful prayer, I called, and my entire set of keys had been returned to the lost and found. I was ecstatic and I knew Whom to thank!

Shortly after my Broncos stadium escapade, I decided to adventure on a camping excursion with friends. My buddy Nate likes trucks—really, really, big and manly trucks—and fun adventure toys, too. One of those was something called a RZR. It looks like a slick and glorified jeep made for four-wheeling. We took it up steep climbs and down hills that looked like the drop from the top of a rollercoaster. I'm not sure how we didn't fall out, but I guess that's why RZR gets the big bucks.

After our grand adventures on the RZR, hiking, and camping, we loaded up Nate's truck, complete with snacks and country tunes for the ride home. Nate is a thoughtful guy, and he didn't want to disrupt our ladies' sing-along to the country countdown, so he sacrificed his spare key to keep the music streaming in the truck as he and the guys hitched up his RZR before heading back down the bumpy mountain road.

At least twenty miles into the journey, we made a pit stop to drop the RZR back in its RV home. We were all happy-go-lucky after a fiery prayer and country jam session, two of my very favorite things. Hopping out of the truck in laughter, Nate went to reach for his keys only to find the single spare still in the ignition. His original key set *was missing*. He searched the front of the truck, the console, and the back seats. *Nothing.* We couldn't find his key ring with the special RZR key *anywhere*. He summoned a search party with all five of us looking high and low. And still, *nothing*.

"We must've left them back up at St. Mary's Glacier," Nate said in a semi-frightened voice.

Still dancing to the beat of my own drum, I refused to believe we had left the keys behind. And I know it sounds crazy, *but even if we had, I believed Jesus could bring them back* because of my recent experience at the Broncos game. If my keys were returned from a stadium filled with 77,000 people, we could get Nate's keys back, too! The faith from my past experience gave me a foundation to draw from to believe for faith in that current moment. I *knew* that God would make a way. I just knew it! I guess that's what a mustard seed of faith looks like. Thank goodness God says He can work with such a small amount. Faith needs action, so I started a conversation with the Lord and invited my friends to join by praying together aloud. I asked the Lord if He would please return the keys in whatever fashion He chose. We continued praying while circling the truck multiple times as we asked the Lord to reveal the keys.

Still *nothing.*

We searched for about thirty minutes before half of the team started to lose hope. I still felt stirred inside, and the silent voice in my head uttered, *Jesus, I believe You are going to make these keys appear, and I want to be the one to find them with You!*

Only seconds later, I looked up, and there, on the back bumper of Nate's gigantic Ford truck, *were his keys.* It looked like someone plopped them down in plain sight, right in the middle of the bumper!

Each one of us let out a little shriek of excitement and relief as we thanked Jesus with a celebratory dance. Instead of singing to them, we now looked like the lyrics of a country song two-stepping and hootin' and hollerin' in the RV parking lot. The guys, still very much in shock, unlatched the RZR, and *finally,* we were on our way home.

The entire trip back, we talked about the impossibilities of the keys riding on the truck bumper for twenty miles on the bumpy, dirt-caked mountain road, followed by the high speed of 65 on the highway. *There was just no way.* And even if they had survived the trek, we all diligently looked for the keys in every corner and crevice of the truck for *thirty minutes*. All five of us! Then, suddenly, they appeared on the back bumper in plain sight after agreeing in prayer for Jesus to make them appear. To this day, we joke about an angel sitting on the back bumper safeguarding and twirling the keys around his finger, kicking his legs back and forth, and laughing all the while. Oh, what a joy it is to see things from heaven's perspective.

CHAPTER 9

SURE AS THE SHORE

*T*he ocean has always been my happy place. Growing up, we traveled a lot, and my vote was always for the beach. I didn't care which beach. I just needed sand and water. When I can find a way to help people, travel with friends or family, *and* hit the beach, it's the best of all worlds.

One summer, when things were looking grim with my fitness studio, I took a week to pray, serve, and explore partnership with a well-respected anti-trafficking organization in San Jose, Costa Rica. My intern made the connection, the team seemed excited, and my studio needed a transformative makeover, so I committed to the visionary trip down south. The idea was to employ men and women coming out of trafficking as fitness instructors in the studio. The team and I dreamt up all kinds of ideas, one being a trauma-release course through movement. No matter the vision I had premeditated for these trips, the Lord always seemed to blow me away with a surprise agenda of His own.

The work was intense. Halfway through the trip, on a rainy and mundane night, one of the girls in the safe home ran away. The staff and I were up all night, pacing and praying for her return.

She never came back, at least not during my stay there. I could *feel* the spiritual oppression and heaviness blanketing the whole city, especially during "ministry night" when we prayed with men of all races and backgrounds. Some were buyers of sex, and some may not have been. Either way, it appeared most were involved with prostitution and trafficking in some capacity, as they were lingering outside the largest brothel in Central America late into the night.

I'm thankful the Lord teaches us to rest. After the intensity of that week, I needed a couple days on the beach. I sensed the interns and staff needed time off, too. Some of the staff members hadn't been out of the safe house in months! So, when the idea of a beach trip surfaced, ears perked up, and my solo trip turned into me plus four college-aged gals. We packed our bags and meandered over to the bus fare window in the center of the city to practice our Spanish while purchasing tickets. And by "we," I mean my one friend Elise. She was more fluent than any of the rest of us. Yet, not knowing for sure, we prayed and hopped on the three-hour bus which *thankfully* landed us right where we intended. Our first stop: the beach!

That evening before dinner and as girls do, we got dressed up. I overheard one of the girls saying she had not been to the ocean since she arrived in-country, so our special visit prompted a spontaneous photo shoot on the sand before making our way to dinner. All five of us dropped our shoes on the shoreline, climbed across a fallen dead tree branch and posed our little faces off. We got a lot of great pictures that day, *and* a little more than we anticipated.

Dusk hit and so did our hunger pangs. We shuffled our feet over the wet sand on the path back to our shoes. The tide was rising, and the waterline looked as if it had recklessly danced with three pairs of shoes that were now scattered across the sand, but two pairs were nowhere to be found. I guess the ocean has a great sense of fashion because it chose the two brand new and very expensive pairs. We all circled like vultures high up on the shoreline where we tucked away each pair. The two shoeless girls started to have minor panic attacks as they frantically zig-zagged their way along the shore and even searched the incoming waves.

Meanwhile, I pondered with Jesus how I had never experienced His wild and fun faith stories with others, until the keys. I thought to myself, *How could this be any different?* If only these girls could experience the faith miracles I had in the past! Doubt answered back, *But, what if God didn't show up this time? It might hurt these girls.* I was thinking of one in particular who was utterly distressed. And then hope spoke, *"Oh, but what if He did?"*

There was only one way to know. I gathered the five of us to circle up for a family talk with Daddy God in our beach "living room." I remember feeling slightly hesitant with a front row audience to my bold prayers of faith. Yet, I uttered some words about how the Lord created the ocean, and if He created it, He could surely return anything from it. It reminded me of the father in the Bible who asked Jesus to heal his son *if* He was able. And Jesus replied, "Everything is possible for one who believes" (Mark 9:23). I felt so much like the dad as I was saying the words in faith and feeling the doubt lingering as I tried to push away the unbelief and lack of hope swirling around us.

Twenty minutes of searching went by, and darkness fell making it nearly impossible to continue the hunt. The girls came walking up to me with blank stares. My thought from the looks of their faces was, *Oh no, Lord, why?*

But my intern Caitlyn said, "We got them. All of them. Some sweet man said they washed up on shore, all four of them together, and he asked if they were ours!"

I was awestruck. It was a miracle! All four shoes washed ashore *together* after being in the ocean for over *twenty minutes!* I couldn't understand why the girls weren't more ecstatic. And then it dawned on me: either they were in utter shock, *or* they believed it to be mere coincidence.

It can be overwhelming to think the Lord of all creation would listen to a miniscule prayer about material possessions. But it was also a prayer that meant *everything* to our hearts in that moment, and the Lord is in the "heart business." From what I have seen, if He can show us intimacy and we invite it, He will take the opportunity to meet us every time. The Lord loves nothing more than for our world to slow down so He can meet us in the moment to *show us* how involved He really is. He also loves when we give credit where credit is due, and in this case, credit was definitely due after all four shoes took a twenty-minute swim in the rolling waves during high tide.

Once reality hit and our group recognized the Lord's hand in our photoshoot fiasco, we all hugged and stood on the shore thanking Him profusely. Let's just say "the shoe miracle" was the topic of conversation at the dinner table that night. With a whole world of people and craziness going on, it's a wonder Daddy God would look down on five young gals in Costa Rica and wink as He nudged the four tiny shoes ashore. But then again, no dad likes to see his little girls running shoeless around a foreign country. I guess that's what any loving father would do.

*Capturing memories with the ladies in Costa Rica,
probably around the time our shoes were
"borrowed" by the ocean.*

TRAIT IV

OUR BIGGEST FAN

CHAPTER 10

FREEBIES

*J*t's rare to find friends who champion you in every area of life. Quite honestly, I don't expect that from anyone because it would be exhausting to keep up, for them and for me. Yet, if you have been fortunate enough to walk through your deepest pains and greatest accomplishments with a dear friend, hang onto them, and don't let go. There is something special about walking through the hard times and the exciting big achievements with someone who has been walking alongside you through *everything*. It's a gift to be able to go to someone who already knows the hurts, frustrations, and fears and how to overcome those to find incredible joy. Friendship is one of the greatest joys.

Another fun joy is receiving a gift from someone when it's exactly what I needed or had been asking Jesus for. It's one of the most powerful ways to my heart. Most of the time, it's not the gift itself that's winsome, but it's how the gift makes me feel seen and heard. If you've ever read *The Five Love Languages*, this story may help you to understand the "gift giving" love language at its core. I don't consider "gifts" one of my top love languages with people; but with the Lord, I love knowing He hears me. I love knowing that I'm on His mind. So, when I talk with the Lord throughout my day, about the big things like abolishing sex trafficking and victim mindsets to the smaller things like wanting a new rug for my kitchen, it's always good to know I'm not talking to a wall. To feel heard is one of the greatest treasures in friendship. It builds trust. And a history of well-built trust is the strongest foundation for real faith.

I've never met a better listener than Jesus. Even if He seems silent, delayed, or right on time, He's always listening. I know because I like to pray the fun prayers as well as the difficult ones—the "not my will, but Yours be done" kind of prayers—because I trust Him with every fiber in my being. I trust the Lord so much that sometimes He has to give me a kick in the pants and tell me to trust myself because we are one, I in Him and He in me.

I used to do a lot of fit modeling for outdoor companies, mostly behind the scenes. Several of the companies were big names, but I basically stood in a large conference room as people doctored up the fit of the item I was wearing. There were so many blessings that came with the jobs, including free workout clothes for over ten years of my life. The teams gifted me everything from sports bras and socks to shirts, leggings, and bags. My family and friends got to reap the benefits, too! I was thankful for every single item, even the ones I gave away.

After college, I had entered into a chapter in life where I lived in my parents' basement and was unemployed for four months (other than occasional modeling gigs). I had spent every day crying out to the Lord, asking for next steps in a career. *I was my career.* Success *was* my identity, and being financially stable was all I knew. I don't fault anyone in my life for it. In fact, stability is a major blessing! I just thought I was a failure for being let go from my very first paid internship as a sales representative in the beer industry. As it turned out, I didn't like it anyway.

The waiting season can be just as hard as the grinding seasons, if not harder. I spent every day for eight hours or more with an open Bible and open laptop as worship sets played on repeat. I made list after list of what I thought were perfect jobs and asked the Lord for all of them. "Strong Enough" by Matthew West was my daily jam as my heart ached and my soul wept at the feet of the Lord. I applied to jobs here and there, but ultimately, the Lord was the One who knew my next steps, so I figured applying blindly to jobs made little sense when He already had all the answers. Little did I know that season of life would be the foundation on which I built my faith.

When I was asked to model sporadically throughout that chapter of life, it was a wonderful and invited interruption to my daily cry fests. One morning, I woke up for a run and threw on my favorite Nike running leggings I had owned since high school (and the only pair I had ever purchased myself). Eight years later, the elastic had completely worn through to make them nearly see-through. Even my frugal mind knew it was time to retire them. I was sad to see them go because they held so many memories from track in high school and race days with Dad. I remember saying to Jesus, "I'm getting rid of these in faith, Lord. Please honor my decision to invest in myself." I planned to get new ones later that week.

The next day, I was scheduled to model with Sports Authority at its corporate office. I tried on everything from sports bras to tank tops to leggings. I always loved seeing what would be coming out on the market in a year and a half. The session was like any other, and before picking up my bag to leave, one of the gals tossed me some clothes and said, "Here, you can take these home." In the mix were a sports bra (which I also needed) and not one, but *two* pairs of leggings, three-quarter length *and* full length. Remembering the prayer I had prayed the day before, I got teary-eyed and overwhelmed with thankfulness.

God makes a way and pushes beyond rules and regulations. Sports Authority had a mandate from corporate to never give away samples because they had to repurpose and save fabrics by sending them back to the factory. But Jesus is faithful! I'll be honest in saying the leggings I received weren't as cute as my ten-year-old ones I tossed the day before. But I learned a lot in that moment—it's not about the gift itself. It truly wasn't. It was about the step of faith I took. And God responded. I felt heard. I felt seen. And I felt deeply loved by Him.

I look back, and I am glad I didn't get "the best of the best" leggings that day because the reality is we can't always get what we want. I think there's a song about that. And thank goodness we don't! Have you ever met kids with parents who gave them everything they ever wanted, and when they didn't get their way, they screamed in horror as if their lives were ending? I don't want to be one of those. I don't think you do either. There's a balance, however. We can learn to value and love ourselves the way the Lord loves us. We can learn to ask. We can learn to invest in ourselves (or in others if we have spending issues). We can learn to receive His gifts with open hands and hearts.

We only have the ability to love others with the depth that we understand love for ourselves. And we only know *how to love* because Jesus shared His capacity of love for us. He is the sole reason we are able to experience love. It's what scripture means when it says, "We love because He first loved us" (1 John 4:19).

At that point in my life, I had a hard time loving myself and investing in myself financially. I was taught "the frugal way is the only way." Jesus taught me, "I am a God of abundance. I am

Provider, and I honor your step of faith." So, the truth is, the leggings themselves weren't the greatest blessing that day. The blessings came through my lessons of loving myself enough to invest in my wellbeing, trusting the Lord as Provider in my season of lack, and being seen and heard by my Friend, Jesus, in a difficult time.

The Lord transforms us if we allow Him. My heart-shift in that season was the greatest gift I could have ever received as an unemployed twenty-one-year-old. We *must* go through the stripping for the rebuilding to take place, even if it starts with a simple task like tossing out some old leggings. It's the lasting joys of self-love and friendship with God that help us to see beyond the deep and treacherous waters in the now, because the now won't last. But the memories on which we build solid foundations *will*.

It would take a separate book to cover the sheer number of items the Lord has given me, things I've asked for as well as some complete surprises. I don't say that to boast but to testify to His goodness and to encourage others in their faith. God tells us we do not have because we do not ask. I just take Him at His word, and I know that's an invitation for all of us! From my experience, it's less about the item and more about the intention and heart of the Father behind it. I'm still unwrapping some of those "unseen" gifts from the items I've received to this day!

CHAPTER 11

ROOTING US ON

$\mathcal{I}$’ve always had secret desires in my heart that I’ve wanted to accomplish at some point in my short time on this earth. It’s fun to have a Best Friend who can also read my every thought because one of those secret desires was to complete a triathlon. The problem was I had a deeply-rooted fear of biking. Yes, riding a bike intimidated me. My fear most likely stemmed from a silly experience in college when a homeless man scolded me for biking on the sidewalks in Boulder. I was a people-pleaser and felt the shame immediately crumble any love I had for biking. After that experience, I vowed the sport wasn’t for me.

That aside, I wanted to do a triathlon, which meant I *had* to bike. My best friend was a natural, having completed a *full* Ironman. We used to pedal here and there together, but it wasn’t until I got a nudge from the Lord to conquer my fear of biking that I really committed to training. My best friend aided in the process by providing the perfect bike. There are perks to having friends who are about the same height and size as you are!

My side hustle in modeling was yet again another blessing in this season. As my name spread in the active modeling world, I found myself working with Specialized, a top biking brand. I was also asked to do a photo shoot with a local biking company where they gave me free reign to choose any item I wanted to take home. I chose biking shorts (because we all know biking without those pads in the shorts can be brutal). The biking shorts weren't quite enough to get me to join a race, but they did get me out on the bike a bit more. Soon after, I received a cute, blue-patterned triathlon "kit" as they call them. It was a two-piece, and yet again, I brushed my dream aside and continued to use the cute gear for personal rides around Cherry Creek Reservoir with my roommates.

Apparently, I wasn't getting the message from the Lord after those two gifts, because when I told the fit ladies from Specialized I was training for a triathlon (though I had not fully committed in my mind), they went ahead and surprised me with a customized kit that only the pro athletes and one other person had—*me*. Yikes! God knew I wouldn't sign up unless He pushed me. And so, the day I got my free triathlon kit was the day I mentally committed and went "all in" on training.

My hesitancy in committing to a race most likely came from my college days when I was crazy enough to complete a full marathon without even trying the half. It was a commitment, all right. I trained for four and a half months leading up to the Denver Marathon. In those long months of training six days a week, I grew to despise the very thing that set me free. Unfortunately, three months after the big race, I didn't even want to *look* at my running shoes. The burnout was real and I couldn't go through that again. This time, I wanted to *enjoy the journey*. What a concept for a personality like mine.

As I mentally committed to the race, I also pledged to train God's way. His way looks like rest and surrender, two words that offend an athlete's mind and vocabulary, yet He made it easy. The only other plan I had for summer besides my race was a trip to Maui and Kona. Maui for a wedding, and Kona to visit friends. It was a welcomed interruption, seeing as I would get my beach fill, and it also seemed to have been a strategic interruption from the Lord.

I was nervous to travel for a week and a half during training, but I figured it wasn't long enough to get "out of shape." When I arrived in Kona, I was greeted by fresh leis, smiling friends, and an abundance of fresh fruit. I made colorful and fresh smoothies from the 'aina every morning followed by a run and swim at the pier. Little did I know, Kona just so happened to be *the* place for the largest Ironman race in the world. I literally had no idea.

My swims in the ocean turned into adventures of snorkeling while training. Fancy that! I got to scope out beautiful blue and yellow fish while preparing for my race. I had such a blast that I extended my stay an extra two weeks and didn't care if it meant heading back to altitude to race the next month. The joy of the process was worth it to me.

Race day arrived, and I must admit the race was tough. I had a minor panic attack in the water. Yet, the biking portion ended up being my favorite part of the entire race! I kept passing people thinking, *Am I missing something? Should I be saving more energy for the run?* as I continued to cruise on by participants. I hopped off the bike and felt the "tree trunk" heaviness in my legs my best friend warned me about as I continued on to the last portion of the race.

Nearing the end of the run, I thought I was going to have to slow down, but I wanted to push through! I prayed for strength and as I did, *He will mount them up on wings like eagles. They will run and not grow weary*, replayed over and over in my head. Right as I started to utter the words aloud, other participants pointed to a tree as they cheered me on toward the finish, saying, "Look! A bald eagle!" Just one. All by itself in a barren tree. Even while typing this, I'm having a revelation of the Father's love. Just like my earthly dad was cheering me on at the end of my marathon, Daddy God was encouraging me and waving me into the finish line of my triathlon. I ended up getting second in my age group!

As with the leggings, the tri-suit was just the cherry on top. The Lord knows every now and again I need a little kick in the pants to face my fears head-on. That custom suit sent with my name on it was the nudge I needed to step out. The bald eagle embodying the Lord's support was the umph I needed to finish. And the surprise training atmosphere of Hawaii was what I needed to learn to enjoy the process. God is so much more than a Provider of things. He cares about our goals, dreams, and the fish we get to see amid life's big ocean reef along the way.

*Riding my way to second place on my borrowed
bike while repping my triathlon suit gifted to me
by the design team at Specialized.*

TRAIT V

DIVINE RECRUITER & CONNECTER

CHAPTER 12

DREAMING WITH JESUS

*T*he concept of entrepreneurship was foreign to me as I had parents who held nine-to-five jobs their entire lives. My grandma was a schoolteacher. One of my grandfathers was a manual laborer, and the other was a college football coach. Yet, I always had this burning desire to create new *anythings* and to dream up better ways of doing *everything*. I lost plenty of sleep in the night due to some good and some not-so-good ideas that came to me on a regular basis. For whatever reason, my creativity seemed to be sparked in the dead of the night.

My first entrepreneurial endeavor was in college when a friend and I started a management club. It ended up being a bit of a bust, seeing as the guys showed up just to stare at the ladies and hope to land a date. We *did* raise money for a nonprofit and hold management panels in the downturn of the economy. We also ate some great cheese and pepperoni pizza. At the very least, it was a good resume-builder and stomach-filler during the long study hours. I learned a lot of what not to do, which I hear is one of the best lessons in life.

It wasn't until losing that first job in the beer industry where I finally learned to surrender—like truly let go in my very core. The days were long but seemed short as I poured out my heart before the Lord, nearly begging Him to open a door, but not just any door, one that related to the desires of my heart. The Lord knew I couldn't bring myself to work in another beer sales environment again.

I applied to jobs that only led to closed doors. I was prayerful about where to apply, and each time I talked myself into the excitement of the job, yet another door would close. It didn't make sense.

"Why God?" I would cry out. "I'm a hard worker. I'm trustworthy, diligent, personable. I just don't understand."

During that time, I decided to start volunteering in places that brought me joy. One was a homeless shelter in downtown Denver. The other was a nonprofit that shipped, donated, and repurposed medical supplies to clinics in developing countries, *and* it just so happened to be only fifteen minutes from my parents' house. The CEO had spoken to one of my college business classes. I must have kept his business card because I tracked him down to find out more about his organization.

As it turned out, they only had 20 staff and 17,000 volunteers, so I knew that a paid gig was out of the picture, yet they welcomed me with open arms as a volunteer. It was a cool organization, and I met a girl my age who took me under her wing. She taught me everything she knew. We went to lunch together, and I helped her with reports. I got to know the office and staff well. It was exactly what I needed to stay busy and yet rest at the same time in that season of unemployment.

When I wasn't crying out to the Lord or modeling, I was pouring into those two organizations. I met a lot of amazing people at the homeless shelter, too. One of them told me I looked like Britney Spears when wearing my hat as I dished out pasta. It was a nice compliment seeing as I was a 90s kid, and it brought me a smile in my seemingly unending season of unemployment.

I enjoyed listening to people's stories, feeling productive, and being "seen" by others in a really difficult time. I think we all like to feel seen. It's part of our humanness and how we're wired. But that was also my problem. I didn't feel seen by the Lord. Though I could feel His peace and nearness, I didn't feel heard.

I felt abandoned in the deepest pit while living in my parents' basement as a recent graduate with no job, applying to many jobs, only to be rejected over and over. Each one hurt, especially the rejection of applying for a grant writing position at the medical nonprofit I grew to love. Because I was a volunteer, I had an "in" and already knew the staff. *If I couldn't hold my first job or get hired at the nonprofit, who would want me?* I wondered. The lies all started to seep in.

I didn't know it at the time, but I was learning to battle through prayer, through worship, and through health. Journaling was part of my worship. It's how I expressed myself to the Lord, and it's when I felt the Holy Spirit "huddle up" with me as we mapped out the blueprint for my dream career. I loved the dreaming process. It was the waiting I hated.

Because I am a list gal, I was always updating my lists as I journaled. Each dreaming session, I could feel the Holy Spirit cozying up next to me while lying on our stomachs and kicking our feet in the air, at least that's how I imagined it.

~

The dream career I listed out in my journal read:

1. Related to Africa
2. Help people
3. Work with those impoverished everyday
4. Travel involved
5. Create opportunity for those in poverty
6. Serve them and coach them toward successful futures
7. Sales of some sort/Working with people in the business world
8. Organization with good values/Christian-like vision
9. Located in California or Denver
10. Pays enough that I can live on my own
11. Prepares me for healthcare in Africa

I just *couldn't* understand the delay. And although I thought I trusted God, the jury was still out. Though we had quality and peace-filled, dreaming dates, I had yet to see if He would come through. In the waiting, running was a great outlet during those long months. I don't know what I would have done without it.

One morning, I needed to get out—out of the house, out of my mind—*just out.* So, I threw on my tennis shoes, put in my earbuds, and halfway into my run, I received a call from the CEO of the medical nonprofit. My hands were clammy, and it wasn't from running. I nervously joked about how he must have had a radar for when I was exercising because it was the second time he called during a run. He laughed and said that he had some exciting news. His nonprofit was creating a new position, and he thought I would be a great fit. He continued to explain that the job would entail overseeing all six of their programs, which would include sales and working with people in the community. It was a position that required national and international travel, and I would get to exercise my creative and entrepreneurial bone by updating and growing the programs.

I think I skipped the whole way home, not caring what the neighbors thought. I updated my resume right away and went in for a lunch interview that week. Even though some people in the organization saw me as unqualified, the Lord gave me favor with the CEO of the health nonprofit, and I was offered the job!

I went back to my journal to celebrate with the Lord and thank Him profusely. As I did, my eyes were drawn back to my job list. *All eleven items were fulfilled through the brand new position.* Not one was missed. The Lord was working things together on my behalf and preparing the place for me *the whole time.* I just had to wait and, quite honestly, rest.

I look back on that time as a major life lesson. There was a lot of heartache and worry involved in a place where I could have been enjoying four months of vacation and time with my family and friends. I could have been resting and even taking a week to vacation with the free flight passes. I guess we live and learn, right? I can confirm that the tears and pressing in *did* grow my relationship and faith with the Lord. And now, whenever there is a delay, I always go back to my journaling habits, knowing the Lord is working out everything on my behalf— and not just mine but on behalf of others, too. That's the beauty of dreaming with God. He works it all out for the good of everyone. He makes the dreaming process interesting, and if we let Him, dare I say, He makes it *enjoyable.*

CHAPTER 13

BEST FRIEND BLIND DATE

I was typically *that* person who floated from friend group to friend group. I didn't have a best friend, per se, but rather a lot of really good friends. Whether it was my independence or free-spiritedness, I'm not sure, but I didn't seem to have many friends throughout my life who truly *knew* me.

In college, the Lord gave me my first *real* best friend. She taught me people were more than agendas and laughter was medicine for the soul. She marked me forever, and we still talk to this day. We honor and respect our faith differences and varying dreams in our hearts. Hers was to chase the music scene, and mine was to move to Africa. After my earth-shattering dream encounter, I couldn't shake it. I wanted to start an organization similar to my friends' in Uganda, a sustainable nonprofit of sorts. But back then, I didn't have the right motives. I wanted all the glory and kudos for myself. I wanted the credit *and* the accolades. I'm not proud of it now, but it's the truth. Either way, I had it in my mind to get to Uganda.

I knew, right out of college, I couldn't go straight to Africa with my piles of student loans. That's why when I made "the list" of items I wanted in a stable job and the Lord came through, I was ecstatic! My nonprofit job was an incredible experience, yet still a stepping stone to my greater goal. After three years, I acquired knowledge about business and healthcare in the third world, and I no longer had student loans holding me back, so I decided the time had come to leave. It was time to pursue my original dream to get to Africa.

A couple days before delivering my two-weeks' notice to my boss, I was compiling the necessary emails and contacts for my third trip to Uganda. It was an exploratory trip for a potential business consultant position. Anytime I heard "Uganda," in the office, my ears perked up, and I honed in on the conversation. Our office was small and lined with cubicles, so eavesdropping was the norm. That evening, I was in the office later than usual, and I had plans to meet a friend for dinner. As I was packing up to leave, I heard "Uganda, Uganda, Uganda," sprinkled here and there throughout a conversation in the nearby cubicle.

Bingo. I needed to meet the "Uganda lady." On the way out, I excused my interruption and introduced myself as I told her of my plans to move out there. She said, "Well, I know this is last minute, but our nonprofit is hosting a fundraiser tonight at seven."

The fundraiser was to start in two hours, and I was supposed to meet a friend for dinner. *But, it was Uganda!* I asked my friend if we could reschedule, and I headed home to change for the gala.

I knew no one. Even the lady who invited me couldn't attend, but I didn't care. It felt like a divine appointment, and I was there to connect and learn. As I walked in, I introduced myself to the founders and explained my intention of being a consultant in Uganda for organizations like theirs. They seemed indifferent to the idea as they replied, "You need to meet Sarah! She just moved here a few months ago. She is our Sponsorship Coordinator, and I think you two will really hit it off."

Frustrated that they didn't seem to understand my purpose in being there, I agreed to meet this "Sarah" anyway. I thought she might be an "in" to the organization so that I could help them as a "boots on the ground" contact.

Shortly after talking with the founders, Sarah skipped onstage to deliver her heartfelt sponsorship speech. She seemed more than a little "upbeat" and incredibly smiley. She was cute, but I wasn't in the market for a friend. I needed business clients.

After she got offstage, we chatted a bit, and she said, "Of course I'll reach out! We can grab coffee."

Still frustrated, I couldn't tell if she was taking me seriously and interested in strategizing for our businesses or if she was just looking for friends. I told her I was potentially leaving for Uganda in a little over a month if the finances came through. She replied, "I was looking to go soon, too. We should meet up!" I agreed knowing we could evaluate the needs of their organization in-country together.

A month later, we found ourselves together in Uganda at their nonprofit base, hanging out with children of all ages and eating *chapati*, a fried, sweet, and not-so-healthy, but oh-so-delicious bread. It tastes like a donut without frosting. We navigated some of the trenches of doing business in Africa and shared our hearts with one another. It turned out we did have quite a bit in common—a scary amount, actually. And we just so happened to be navigating similar job territories as she was also praying about moving to Uganda to be the point person for the organization. One thing was sure, if she moved, that meant I was out of the picture as a contestant for business consulting.

Toward the end of our visit, we talked ourselves into a self-care night to retreat from the hustle, dirt, and cold showers at the children's home. We splurged on a two-story hotel room with stone showers and hot water. The hotel even offered a balcony that overlooked Lake Victoria. After soaking in our luxurious steam showers, we put on pajamas and made our way out to the balcony and shared our hearts.

Sarah was walking through the same boy circumstances that I was. We were both navigating the big move to Uganda. We both had a passion for health and fitness. Little did we know, this was a blind date, ordained in heaven by the Lord of the Universe. He knew that I needed a best friend who could understand me in every way—one who would later walk through the exact circumstances I was walking through in the same season, and one I could pray with and go to war with on our knees.

If you've read the scriptures about David and Jonathan, our friendship became like that. I always tell people these many years later that Sarah is "my Jonathan." Only the Lord could have knit together such a deep friendship. We talk regularly to this day. And she still reminds me how she won. I thought I was getting a business client, and she thought she was getting a best friend. I know we are both competitive, but this is one instance where I'm thankful I was wrong.

CHAPTER 14

AIRPORT CONNECTIONS

*A*s you know by now, I love airports. Yes, for the adventure. Yes, for the travel and experience. But the best reason is the divine appointments with Jesus *and* with people. I've had a lot of spontaneous "God-scheduled" meetings in terminals and on planes, but my favorite appointment was when I met Beverly.

It was the same trip out to Uganda with my friends from ROWAN. I flew standby to Newark and Brussels with my friends on the same flights! Thanks to my donor in Colorado, I also had a purchased and secure ticket from Brussels to Uganda. The purchased ticket meant I needed to re-check my bags through customs in the Brussels airport. My friends streamlined their bags straight to Uganda, and in the customs scramble, I was separated from the group, which was a stressor since my phone was nearly dead. With my charger packed in a large sea of clothes, I found myself wishing I had charged my external battery ahead of time. I started to get a bit hot and flustered. That's why, when Bev's sweet voice broke my anxious flurry, I felt immediate relief.

I soon discovered Bev was an American from Florida. I told her I grew up in Colorado, and I think she mentioned she had family there, but I really don't remember. Everyone always seems to have an auntie, cousin, or uncle with only one degree of separation to Colorado. It seems to be a common state to live in for a short time.

In the endless line of people surrounding us, I asked where she was traveling, and when she said, "Uganda," I knew this was no longer a flippant conversation but a God-appointed one. I laughed and told her I was also going to Uganda with all my friends who were already sitting at the gate. She continued on about how she started an organization a year prior, but they were struggling with a lot of corruption within their Ugandan staff. One of my favorite "giftings" the Lord passed down to me is acting as a connector. I immediately exclaimed, "You need to meet my friend Kelsey at the gate! She's been running a nonprofit in rural Uganda for eight years."

As we were talking, I saw her rummaging around in her bag, soon pulling out an external battery charger. Looking at my battery with one percent remaining, I asked if I could borrow it while waiting in the stagnant line. She smiled and beamed in her cute Southern accent, "Oh, you can just borrow it and give it back to me at the gate."

We checked our bags and parted ways. The "cloud nine" feeling from getting the last seat and overhead bin space returned. I found my mind shooting up a question to Jesus about what else He had planned on this wild and crazy adventure.

When we got to the gate, Kelsey and Bev connected and shared stories. They exchanged contact information, and that was that. It was a brief, yet wonderful two-hour journey of getting to know my new friend Bev and then parting ways as the crew welcomed us onto the plane.

That trip to Uganda was powerful. We were greeted on the red dirt road by kids and women dancing, singing, and waving palms. I cried. My heart desires dance and song more than anything, and it was so overwhelming I couldn't hold back my emotions. Dance is the way the Lord romances my heart the most. They made us feel like royalty. One of the guys in our group got out of the van to dance in the street *with* the kids. We all followed suit. I'm forever marked by that memory, truly one of the top five in my life.

During one of our "play days" with the kids, we painted a rainbow-esque mural on the side of a building between spontaneous dance sessions while throwing the kids on our shoulders. It was a good time. Our times of rest came as we listened to people's hearts as they shared their life stories. One afternoon, we did house visits with the pastor of the town and prayed with sick widows who had contracted AIDS and who were completely ostracized by their community. I couldn't believe these sweet women would be left alone to die by themselves in their dung huts covered by grass roofs. I loved watching Pastor Paul love them well and invite us into their stories.

My business mind couldn't help but admire the "savings groups" one of the local pastors of ROWAN started. The Ugandan community members gathered weekly into groups of no more than ten people and collected one another's money to save toward their dreams. They were essentially one another's banking system, and they created their own rules for the group. They even had different "key holders" to protect each other from theft. A woman in the group shared a story about how she saved enough money to buy a goat, sold the goat, and then bought a cow. With the money from selling milk and the cow, she was able to purchase land and start a rental property! The model was working, and it was my heart's deepest desire to see more of these stories come to life!

I returned from that trip without clarity of a defined job, but with more hope I would be returning to live in Uganda very soon. I settled in and began to connect further with the Ugandan nonprofit owners over the coming weeks. When I circled back with Kelsey, I was caught off guard when she texted, "Actually, what are you doing tomorrow? Do you want to come to a meeting with Beverly and me? Remember Beverly from the airport? She's in Colorado."

I thought to myself, *Yes! What kind of meeting? But whhhhhhat will I wear?* as the voice of the Grinch floated across my mind. I smirked as I made an internal joke with myself in such a time of unknown circumstances.

My actual response to Kelsey was, "I'd love to! Please send the address. I'll see you tomorrow!"

The next day, I walked into an elegant office across from the Rockies stadium in downtown Denver. It was paneled with dark wood, and the majority of the walls were lined with glass windows. *I'm glad I dressed up*, I thought to myself as I walked into a large conference room with a huge oval table and four brand-new faces I did not know. I introduced myself with a nervous smile thinking, *Jesus, You've really outdone Yourself this time. Where am I, and who are these people?*

In walked Beverly. *Phew!* I was thankful to know at least two people. She gave Kelsey and me a hug as she sat down at the table. Joining us last was a businessman who looked very important and "in charge." And he was.

It turned out this business office belonged to Beverly's brother, Stan. He was a big-time "Kingdom businessman" in the Denver community. He proceeded to get out his keyboard and projector and dove right into his biblical business model of giving back 20 percent of profits to the community through their nonprofit, which his sister, Beverly, oversaw. It was all making sense.

I secretly high-fived Jesus, and my heart was sent into a flutter as Stan further explained his business model. It was the *exact* model the Lord had been highlighting to me throughout my whole trip to Uganda! Everything the Lord showed me about for-profit businesses funding nonprofits was literally being explained on a whiteboard and with a structure that worked! He continued to talk about a conference his company was conducting in December of that year, where millennial entrepreneurs were invited to a "Shark Tank" of sorts to submit their business plans.

Stan later became my business mentor, and I was thankful to have several minutes with him, let alone several meetings. Over the coming months and in my waiting time in the lobby prior to our meetings, his assistant repeatedly invited me to her husband's new church in Denver. It wasn't until three months and two business meetings later that I finally walked into the doors of the church and found my new home and community for the next four years. It also turned out Stan was a pretty big deal in the community, too. I was honored the Lord saw me as qualified enough to talk business with such an influential Kingdom businessman. To this day, I'm thankful for the friendship and mentorship I have with Stan and his wife, Cindy.

Even without meeting Bev in the airport, I think we could have eventually crossed paths since we ran in the same circles. Or maybe we wouldn't have. Either way, I love the Lord's creative connections. He could have easily introduced me to Bev and Stan by having me bump into them at a deli in Colorado. But He didn't. The Lord loves to be glorified, and the more I get to know Him, the more I see that life is one big scavenger hunt after another where we get to follow His breadcrumbs.

It's why I leave the storytelling up to Him. I'd much rather meet my mentor and new friend through a customs conversation in the Brussels airport than in my own back yard in Denver. God is fun, and He always works everything together for the good of those who love Him. That's one of my absolute favorite aspects of "The Ultimate Connecter." He's sees it *all*, knows us all, and He makes things happen for the best of everyone involved. That's the kind of leader I want to follow.

*Playing with paint and posing in front of our mural
with part of the ROWAN team in Uganda.*

TRAIT VI

OUR ULTIMATE BUSINESS PARTNER

CHAPTER 15

THE ENTREPRENEURIAL
ROLLER COASTER

I love a good roller coaster. I always have. I just don't love them in the game of life, but I guess that's what you get when you sign up for a life of walking blindfolded with the Lord. Despite the heartaches along the way, I always came out on the other side more beautiful and with the greatest gifts —the ones that matter and last forever—better than any house, car, vacation, or beach. Yeah, I said it—even better than the bluest waters and whitest sand.

This might be one of those chapters that makes you cringe and want to throw in the towel of faith. Just hold on. I don't think the Lord will take everyone to such crazy extremes. Or maybe He will. Who knows? I'm not God. I just *let* Him take over as the Master Planner. I invite Him to do whatever He wants in and through me because I really love and trust Him, and I know He has my best interest in mind, *always*. I believe that for you, too.

It's why I invest so deeply in relationships with a core group of women around the world. We walk through the ups and downs of life *together*. Community is extremely powerful and impor-tant. When the world speaks the opposite, we need friends who remind us He *is* on our side more than we could ever know. He *is* fighting our battles, and He *is* for us and in love with us, even on our ugliest and worst days.

Two and a half years into owning my fitness business and six studio locations later, I finally landed at a studio in south Denver that seemed to get enough of a following to cover expenses. I was living in my community house of women at the time, which was the biggest blessing after pulling thirteen-hour days and being greeted with a plate of fresh-cooked meat and veggies at the end of the night.

Though I wasn't collecting a paycheck yet, *I was* building systems to train up other instructors in body, soul, and spirit. The long hours for no pay were worth it to me because the women were worth it to me. We took weekend retreats and had instructor check-ins quite often. We became a family, and as with all family businesses, things can get hard. Every day felt like I was pulling teeth trying to spread the word about the business. Though I had perpetual conversations with others who mentioned hearing of our studio one way or another, I couldn't seem to get people excited enough to walk through our doors. It felt defeating because we were competing with every big-box studio in Denver that had more instructors and a wider variety of class offerings.

When times got tough, I leaned on my passion and the Lord to get me through. I constantly had to recount how my vision and excitement for the fitness studio actually began in Africa. It all started after leaving my nonprofit job and with my return to my favorite continent. I was tasked to complete several hospital assessments, this time as a volunteer. This trip was one of those prepaid, five-star hotel experiences. The deal was this: My former medical nonprofit employer flew me to Mozambique on the dime of USAID as the sponsor, and I, as a representative of the nonprofit, assessed and drafted reports for twelve hospitals and clinics in return. The stats found their way into very important nationwide documents for the different countries we visited. No pressure as a young twenty-something, right? At the time of that trip, I was also working part-time with a missions organization. We came to an agreement that, if the volunteer opportunity with the medical nonprofit was paying, I could double-up on my efforts and extend the trip to meet with some of the business missionaries from the missions organization in Maputo, the capital city.

These forerunner missionaries were brilliant. They started a gym in the thick of the bustling city that employed street boys. I had never seen such a powerful and sustainable model! They helped boys, ages five to their teens. The boys had a wide array of stories, but most were hooked on every drug they could get their hands on, and as a last resort, they would find and huff glue. They were typically uneducated runaways who would steal, even from one another, to make a living. It was a common occurrence. I can't imagine those daily conversations between best friends, "Bro, is that my five dollars?" as another pockets it as his own. Did they play practical jokes on one another with the "Look! A plane" trick while pocketing the cash? The concept was so foreign to my American mind. Regardless, the boys stole, and it didn't matter from whom.

The gym model really worked, though. The staff members immersed themselves in the culture. They learned the language and lived among the boys. They walked many of the guys into sobriety and saw successes in giving them a solid education, discipleship, and fitness training. It wasn't an easy sequence, but the success stories were worth it.

Many of the boys didn't have motivation to show up to school, so the organization learned to bribe them with a meal if they attended the entire class. Some boys stayed. Others left. Some set goals, worked hard, and even became trainers at the gym! Being that my heart was for sustainable community development in developing nations, I loved this business-as-mission model. I figured I could replicate this fitness concept in Uganda, where I had lasting relationships and connections, or at home in Colorado. The two options couldn't be more opposite. One was an adventure more than a world away where nearly everyone had different colored skin than me. The other was familiar, suburban, *and boring.*

Knowing the Lord had already shut the doors to Uganda twice, and that I would have to jump through fire hoops to register a business in Uganda, I settled on Colorado. I only had to pay a small fee of $50 and fill out a ten-minute one-paged form to register a business in the States. We have so much opportunity in America! With a newly registered business, I was off and ready to fly high on the road to success after receiving countless confirmations to start a missions-driven fitness business.

My whole first year in business was brutal. If I had known ahead of time, I would *not* have started. Not a chance. I'm sure a lot of entrepreneurs would say the same. That is probably the reason God doesn't show us the end before we get there, because otherwise we might never begin.

I often woke up around five or six in the morning after finishing my days at midnight. I wore all the hats (both figuratively and literally to cover my unshowered and greasy hair). I eventually brought on a business partner, but she was a newlywed working full-time *and* finishing school. Though she had a dance background that I thought was perfect for our niche fitness focus, she eventually stepped away in less than a year.

It was a lonely journey with a lot of letdowns. A lot of "Yes, I will be there on Monday" followed by a room of empty promises. Toward the beginning, I was driving to an empty studio six times a day. Each time I would clean, tidy up, write a Bible verse or "quote of the day" on the mirror, and wait in anticipation, only to experience another letdown. In between classes, I posted on social media and pushed new marketing deals to try to get someone, *anyone*, in the door. I aimed to appear successful (as I think many businesses do at the beginning), but I knew I was faking it.

My insecurities and vulnerabilities opened me up to the lies of the enemy: *You're not worth showing up for, or else people would be here. You're never going to cover your costs. You're a failure.* And once I believed one lie, I started to believe them all. I hadn't yet learned to silence the lies. The mental battle began.

Year two was better but still hard. I started to get a following, but I ended up changing locations several times based on demand and feedback from clients. Schedules are fickle, and people have pets and children with last-minute appointments. I learned to grow thick skin, but I think with that skin grew a little bitterness and resentment. I was hurt by God, by people, and by myself for not "doing more" and "trying harder." It was an unhealthy cycle that almost took me out.

At the core, I felt *betrayed*. I thought to myself, *If the Lord led me to it, He will bring me through it.* And I thought the *through it* meant I would own the largest, Christian fitness studio in the world because that's what I asked from Him *in faith*. And up to that point, the Lord had always come through *just* as I had asked. Blind faith, right there. I even declared my future success from the pulpit.

I'm not a quitter, so I kept going, despite the heartache and growing more and more bitter all the while. It wasn't until I started praying for business strategy for our 2019 calendar year (the same time I made the declaration from the pulpit) that I started to get answers. Yet God answered things quite differently than I expected. Very odd, indeed. Most business partners sit down to whiteboard, research competitors, and break out Excel spreadsheets to forecast for the coming year. Not Jesus. Despite the amount of whiteboard sessions I tried to lead, whenever I sat down with Him to plan, all I saw was Mickey Mouse. You read that right. I still laugh about it. I would pray and pray and diligently pray some more. The more I prayed, the more Mickey showed up—everywhere. God likes to speak to me through repetition.

One evening of repeated Mickeys, I walked into Target and saw yet another Mickey. It was on a child's shirt, and I saw it as we both walked through the automatic doors. Directly after, I stopped by my friend's place to meet her new baby, only to find him wearing Mickey diapers (which she said they had never bought before). Then, the next morning I drove to my parents' house to check in for a quick hello (and of course a snack). I peeled back a layer of a banana while asking about my mom's day as I removed a sticker with the face of Mickey staring back at me. It was comical and even a little bit creepy. I felt as if someone were pranking me. Sometimes life with the Lord can feel like one big practical joke.

I'm sure you're thinking, *Mickey is everywhere. Disney is really good at marketing, and I see Mickey often, too.* I'm sure that's what my parents still think to this day. What I know for sure is that this next story is not fabricated in the slightest, and I took a picture to prove it. All I knew then was God was trying to tell me something, and He had me leaning in, all eyes on Him.

CHAPTER 16

OPERATION DISNEY

*T*he greatest secret I learned as Jesus' business partner was *rest*. He rested after creating the world, and if He wanted to model that to us, I figured it was probably important, and I needed to prioritize it, even in business. After all, God runs the world, which is much larger than any Fortune 500 company.

Periodically, I found ways to get away for the weekend to a beach, even while running my business. It wasn't out of the question for me to fly to Hawaii for the weekend. I had a friend who had moved to Oahu and extended the invitation to hike waterfalls and hop waves with her in the midst of facing hard life challenges. I needed a retreat away and she needed a friend to fight some battles by her side. The problem was, the only dates she had available fell right before my proposed trip to Orlando for my "business strategy" meeting with Jesus at Disney World. I wanted to be obedient to hear what the Lord was saying to me with all the Mickey appearances, so that trip was a definite "yes" on my calendar. When God says, "Go," I don't ask questions. *I just go.*

I found a way to get my fitness classes covered by another instructor at our studio, and though I felt a bit guilty for taking two back-to-back trips to the beach, I knew the Lord was repetitively speaking "rest" and "Disney." The trip to Honolulu was rather exhausting. I did a lot of battling and warring in prayer over my friend and her circumstances, and I'm thankful I was able to cover her in prayer because *that's what friends do*. And as the Lord does, He worked it all for good because I got filled up through rest on the beach and the plane ride home. After all, airports are my sanctuary with Jesus.

Sunday was supposed to be my last day in Hawaii. I needed to get back in time for my Monday class only to turn around and leave for Orlando the next day. My friend offered for me to stay and fly straight to Orlando from Hawaii. That would have entailed cancelling my class, as I couldn't get the Monday class covered. I often fill car time with prayers, so as my friend and I were out driving, we both asked the Lord for direction about whether I was to return to Colorado. Before even saying *Amen* in my head, I opened my eyes and immediately saw a sign that said, "Revive," in clear sight. Being that "Revive" was the name of my business, I knew I needed to get back to Colorado and the studio.

Flights looked tight on the standby list, so I showed up to the earlier flight routing through Chicago, hoping to get back to Denver. My friend and I said our goodbyes, and I prayed for more plane favor. After all, I had gotten confirmation in the car that I was to return.

I waited. And waited. And waited until it was just me and another guy sitting on the edge of our seats, waiting to hear our names to board. We heard the dreaded, "And that completes our boarding for today. Your names will be rolled over to the next flight."

I sat and asked the Lord what to do for the next four hours before the last midnight flight to Denver. Being that it was only the two of us remaining in the airport with the gate agents, I felt prompted to strike up a conversation. Though I already knew the answer, I asked if he was a standby passenger. He said *yes* and explained his brother had given him passes to fly out to Honolulu. We continued talking, and within the first two minutes of our conversation, in response to something entirely unrelated, he replied, "Yeah, it's almost like standing in line at Disney."

I was hardly phased anymore by the amount of Disney references, but I couldn't help but laugh out loud as I exclaimed, "Are you kidding me? God has been speaking to me through Disney and showing me Mickey Mouse *everywhere* for the last three months! I'm supposed to be leaving for Florida in two days!"

Wide-eyed with excitement, my new friend, Pierre, continued to tell me how he absolutely *loved* Disney, went to Disney college, and proceeded to pull out a stuffed Mickey Mouse in the Honolulu airport terminal! I couldn't believe my eyes. I didn't think you would believe me either, so I snapped a picture to relive the moment. I'm sure he wouldn't mind you writing to him to hear his side of the story either. He's a kind gentleman and an incredible leader who will help change this world for the better.

Pierre excitedly offered, "I have a free ticket that expires at the end of the month that I won't be able to use. Do you want it? I'm almost positive it's transferable!"

Little did Pierre know, I hadn't bought a hotel, ticket to Disney, or rental car for my Florida trip due to lack of finances and, more importantly, due to lack of a final confirmation from the Lord to "go." I realized it was an extreme risk to travel to Disney so spontaneously since people tend to plan years in advance, yet I believed if the Lord was in it, He would make a way. And He answered me in that moment through Pierre's kindness.

The Lord met us in the airport that night. We found ourselves talking about Jesus and sharing our stories during the four-hour wait for the next flight to Denver. Pierre shared how his dad pastored a church in Chicago. I also learned that he didn't believe he could follow God *and* pursue his dream of acting and screenwriting at the same time. Somewhere along the way, he had been told that the two conflicted with each other. The devil is a liar! And that's exactly what I told him because film culture *needs* lovers of Jesus to influence that lens of the world just as much as any other. I told him God was his biggest Champion because I had *seen* God do amazing things in my own life. (Pierre, I hope the triathlon suit chapter blesses you!) We ended our night praying on the airport floor together while Daddy God poured out His love over Pierre and big tears streamed down his face. I could see Pierre encountering the heart of the Father, and the truth *was setting him free.* Chains were breaking, the same way they had for me so many times before. Pierre physically *looked* lighter.

I never did make that second flight. Sitting on the airport floor that night, praying with Pierre was exactly where I wanted to be, and exactly where God wanted me. Sometimes God can show us a sign to lure us in, but the end goal in our mind isn't the destination. It's why we get to keep checking in with Him to follow His lead, moment by moment and day by day.

And though the ticket was a sweet and incredible gift from Pierre and the Lord, it didn't even compare to the greater gift of seeing Pierre *encounter* the Father's heart. Daddy God showed me firsthand how my time with Pierre was much better than any ride I'd ever take in a theme park, *and* how to relinquish control of my expectations along the journey to get there. The Lord cares so much about each of His sons and daughters that He would chase us down anywhere in the world for just a brief moment with us. *He is in the details.*

Two days after church on the airport terminal floor, I found myself at the Disney entrance with a ticket in hand as I was admitted into the parks. Though I was looking for a glaring sign, nothing crazy happened. I realized the Lord had something much different for me this time around. His message was simple: *play.* I'm realizing, more often than not, I just need to let my hair down on Mr. Toad's Wild Ride and enjoy the unexpected twists and turns. Unfortunately, in the rat race of trying to decode God and His many Mickey Mouse signs, I missed the simplicity of His message.

And the more I journey with the Lord, the more I am starting to realize when I step into His Director's seat when I'm only meant to be the playwright. I imagine Daddy God sitting back and laughing as He ushers me back into my role. Sadly, I know I missed out on the fullness of joy that day at Disney with my friend who flew halfway across the country to meet me there. I was tirelessly looking around every corner for the next hint the Lord might speak and dashing from line to line when I think He just wanted me to take a pause from the business world, to get out of my head, *and just be a kid for the day.* It often offends my mind how free He wants me to be. Sometimes we need to get out of our own way to walk in the freedom He has for us. Next time, I'll stop searching so hard for answers and leave the business details to Lord while I take another spin on Space Mountain.

CHAPTER 17

CLOSURE

I said goodbye to Mickey and Minnie and made my way up the coast to Jacksonville for a church conference at a friend's church. It was the reason I chose that weekend above any other. The conference was small and powerful. Because I had the option, I debated whether to return home Saturday or Sunday. I had been traveling for some time, and I was ready to sleep in my own bed, yet there was one night left of the conference. As my friend toured me around the old beach town of St. Augustine, I felt turmoil in my spirit as to whether I should stay or go. The flights looked awful, and knowing my plane favor had departed from me in this season of life, I decided at the last minute to stay one more night.

That evening at the conference, the pastor was speaking on a message I had never heard before. He was talking about how people don't step into their dreams because of the burden of the outcome if it didn't work out. In the pride of my humanness, I started to detach myself from the sermon and talk with Jesus about how it didn't apply to me because I *did* step into my dreams and I *was* walking them out. *Pride.* My pride was getting in the way of hearing the message.

My thoughts about the message swirled, *Lord, I tried to move to Africa twice and had to release that dream, and I have surrendered my fitness studio at least twelve times over the course of the last three years.*

In that same moment, without a doubt in my mind it was God, He corrected me with a strong impression on my heart saying, *But you're still carrying the burden of outcome, Megan.* I even heard Him say my name in a stern whisper in my head, so I knew He meant business. I knew it was time to let go—of it all. With that impression came extreme relief of *finally* letting go. In "creating history" in my relationship with the Lord, I knew that's how He spoke. His strong correction always brought a sense of hope, love, relief, peace, comfort, and/or joy because that is His character. He can't help but be and do who He is.

I wept. No, I sobbed. I'm talking snot tears in a message where everyone else was taking notes and getting inspired to step into their callings. The past three years and everything I had given up for this dream, even other dreams of moving to Africa, were all wrapped up in this still, small voice. Though there was relief, there was extreme and deeply rooted pain. My studio dream died that night, and I think others could feel it around me, possibly because of the uncontrollable sobs. At least four or five people came up to encourage me and pray with me after. Some were words of encouragement that I didn't want to hear, yet their words felt true at the same time. Sometimes the truth does hurt, but that's why we have Jesus. He walks *with* us through it all.

I'm thankful the Lord takes me to the beach when He delivers hard news. It shows the kindness of His heart. I thought I was taking a trip to Disney for business vision, the beach, and a conference. I left with a new friend from the Honolulu airport and a clear directive to close our doors.

I gave our clients at the studio thirty-days' notice prior to final closure. Looking back, I am thankful I chose to sublet studio space month-to-month rather than invest in a brick-and-mortar. Yet, the pain of losing my "child" I had birthed was settling in. It was all I had known for three years. I lost more than $15,000 (all that I had at the time), lots of sweat, lots of tears, and maybe even a little blood, too. Three years of a labor of love evaporated before my eyes in what felt like a moment's time. And all the while, I was pouring into others' lives, and the seeds in my own heart seemed to have withered and needed just as much watering. All at once, the strategies, training systems, programs, and the deepest longings in my heart died. Just like that.

I didn't realize how sick my soul had become by trying to keep "my baby" alive until God called me out of it. And when He did, the surrender felt like relief. It also felt like death at the same time. I'm not sure how that's possible, but that's what rang true for my heart. I had lost my child. I birthed it, prayed for it, and nurtured it day and night for three years straight. It was not easy to give it up. It was a very emotional goodbye with the ladies at the studio. But for the sake of my "driver" personality, the Lord had to release me from it to save me from my own demise.

The Lord saves us from ourselves. It's one of His jobs in being God. He knows when to intervene because He cares about the wellspring of our hearts, if only we would take the time to listen. If you had a business partner growing in bitterness, saw them losing all sense of joy, and losing their thrill of life, wouldn't you call them aside for an intervention? Maybe, maybe not. I guess that's why Jesus makes the absolute best Business Partner. He's not afraid of confrontation and knows when to pull us up from the pit. The truth hurt, but I have a feeling my pain would have been a lot worse had I kept going.

The beauty is the Lord doesn't waste anything—not a single thing. I believe He will somehow redeem my journey in fitness and in business. *I know* He will because I have the most loving and caring Daddy in the whole world, and He just so happens to be in the resurrection business.

*Capturing the moment with Pierre, my generous
Disney friend in the Honolulu airport.*

TRAIT VII
PAPA THE PROVIDER

CHAPTER 18

HEAVEN INVADES THE ER

*H*ealthcare and a car. These were the two things I asked the Lord for when I started my fitness business. I know you aren't supposed to make negotiations with the Lord; well actually, I didn't know at the time, back before I had some years under my belt with Him, but I've learned since then. I do remember reading several places in Scripture where fathers who went before us would plead with the Lord to change His mind. One was Abraham who asked God not to destroy Sodom and Gomorrah if He found even one righteous person in the city. I realize that's an entirely different and more pressing scenario, but nonetheless, it was still a possibility in my mind to be able to sit and have a voice at the table with the Lord. Being a businessperson, that's what I opted for.

Because of His kindness and mercy in growing His children in our faith, He agreed. It's amazing how God meets us where we are in our learning and growth journey. During the three-year business expedition, I made no more than $12,500 total. For you analytical folks, yes, that was before taxes. I was running my full-time business and making sure all my instructors were getting paid before I did. Over the course of my three years in business, I took home a total of two checks that amounted to no more than $300 each.

Finances were tight, but I didn't know any different, so I learned to live on savings from modeling side-gigs and dog sitting jobs that the Lord brought my way. My friends started to joke about the amount of dog sitting jobs I landed. I would be at a new mansion every other weekend, per the Lord's marketing. I didn't give any attention to spreading the word about my house sitting business. In fact, I started to give jobs away to my roommates if the jobs conflicted with my work or travel schedule. The Lord says He will take care of us. I am here to tell you, He does.

The first two years into business, I was healthy as a horse. I don't think I got as much as a hangnail. Definitely no fever or cough. I was tired from the fifteen-hour days, but I could feel the Lord shielding me from any viruses, infections, or wounds. It's not like there weren't opportunities to get hurt. I was just as adventurous as ever, especially the time in Maui when I fell halfway down a shoot to a waterfall and caught myself (or the Lord caught me, rather) on a rock only five feet before the fifteen-foot drop. That was a scary one. My brother and I still talk about it. I had my angels working double-time that day.

The whole first year in my business, I didn't even have health insurance. Then, a friend told me I qualified for Medicaid, so I investigated and found she was right. It took some time for me as a business owner with a business degree to dismantle my pride and commit to filling out the form. I finally submitted and came to find that Medicaid was like royalty treatment. This isn't meant to be political. I just know it was the way the Lord was providing for me at the time of starting my business, and thank goodness I signed up for coverage because my last year of the business was quite the year of hospital visits. I'm thankful the Lord speaks to us through friends and community.

No need to go into an over-share of human anatomy, but my body was bleeding in a way it shouldn't have been. After my annual physical at an urgent care, my nurse said I needed to see a specialist. She set up the appointment for what would be another six-month journey to get fibroids removed from my uterus.

That hospital trip was a fun one. At the time, I was also working with a Christian nonprofit as their influencer. I shared my story with thousands of women through social media and prayed with many of them across the nation who had experienced stories of infertility and trauma. *It was powerful!* I was already spiritually heightened going into the surgery, and apparently anesthesia increases what's already inside us. Coming out of surgery, my nurse laughed, saying all I wanted to do was pray for *everyone* in the ER. News to me. I don't remember a thing. My best friend came by to pick me up, and we were on our way. All doctor's visits, CAT scans, ultrasounds, surgery, and pain meds were covered. Oh, and the fibroids, *gone!* My doctor said it was quite a successful surgery.

The rest of the year seemed rather uneventful, healthwise. One night, I was delving into the Bible, wanting to spend one-on-one time with the Lord before heading over to a friend's house for a Friendsgiving meal. It was a season of retreating to my room to be with Him. I go through ebbs and flows of being social and hiding out with Jesus. It seems He likes to speak in both scenarios. It may be that He met me in both ways because of my "introverted extroverted" self, as I like to label myself, or maybe everyone goes through seasons of being extremely social and then antisocial. Either way, I pried myself out of bed, bundled up, and loaded up the car with my butternut squash soup dish.

I walked into a room full of pumpkin candles, turkey decor, friends, and a large spread of food. It looked like heaven, and still, for some reason, all I wanted to do was be home in bed with my Bible and journal. I squeezed my way out semi-early from the best sweet potatoes, mac-n'-cheese, and turkey spread. Another friend had a similar idea, and we snuck out together without causing a scene. With the recent freezing rain atop mounds of snow, we both dug our heels into the crunchy, crystalized, white mounds as we struggled down the steep driveway. Everything was wet and *slick*. On the way over that night, I had seen at least two cars do a complete three-sixty mid-driving. I hadn't seen anything like it in all my years of living in Denver!

My friend walked me to my car. As I stepped up onto the curb to open my car door and put my glass Tupperware aside, my feet came out from under me, and I was instantly on the ground. I saw streams of red right away. My elbow hurt badly. I looked under my fluffy down jacket to see the damage. Large and small chards of glass were shattered along my sleeve, and the rest of the glass had made its way into my hand and wrist. Only the plastic Tupperware lid survived.

As I saw the blood, the pain began to register, and my brain sent jabs up my entire forearm. My friend calmly helped me walk back inside, knowing we had two nurses who could help with the immediate trauma. I'm thankful for my nurse and doctor friends.

It's fun to see nurses get into "nurse mode." They skipped the whole "intake" process and rushed me straight to the bathroom. One removed the largest glass pieces jutting out from the meaty part of my palm. The other ran water over the wounds to remove the remaining little chards. It burned, and I squealed as they flushed the deep, bright red cuts with alcohol and whatever other burning cleansers they had. After we got the wounds under control and cleaned well, I was given a "to-go" bandage to stop the bleeding until my sweet friend and I got to urgent care.

I'm thankful for good friends. No one likes going to urgent care alone. Two hours after arriving, I was visited by the late-night shift nurse. Her assistant came in, slightly irrigated the wound with very little pressure from the syringe, and she prepared my hand for stitches. In walked the doctor. She said the x-ray machine was down, but that it was my choice as to whether I wanted to get stitched up. Assuming the wound was fully cleaned and seeing the deep cuts, I decided to move forward with stitches. Only $6 later, I was out the door and headed home to my own bed with a wrap around my hand.

After two weeks, my hand still looked a bit like Frankenstein, but that seemed normal for new wounds. What wasn't normal was the large bulge in the lower part of my hand. The little bubble appeared to possibly be a piece of glass trying to escape to the surface. Dang it! I guess I made the wrong decision in getting stitches.

My primary care nurse got me into another specialist and somehow I scored one of the best surgeons in the Denver area. We decided to operate to try to remove any other possible pieces trying to escape to the surface. I needed anesthesia, but this time, only a "block" where they replaced the blood in my arm with anesthesia medicine. I didn't even know that was possible. It turned out it had the same effect though. I didn't remember a thing.

The surgery went great, and this time, instead of praying for everyone, I insisted we all listen to worship music as they performed the surgery. Two weeks later, I removed the cast-like bandage for the "big reveal." The larger wound looked a bit puffy in a good way, because the doctor was using the stitches to bind the wound together for less of a scar. Scars tell stories, but no one likes a big scar in the middle of their hand, or at least, I didn't. At my follow-up appointment, the doctor came in saying, "You're a very spiritual lady."

I still don't know what that meant. I have no idea what took place in that operating room. I guess only Jesus does. Maybe I can ask Him one day when I'm in heaven. I just imagine my angels cracking up as I was drugged up and inviting the doctors to sing in the OR theatre while undergoing an intense surgery. *I wonder if I was singing.* Yikes. I didn't even think about that until writing this. What a sight that would be. Maybe I should ask for security tapes. It could make a good laugh one day.

I didn't pay a cent for that surgery. I am thankful I live in a country that takes care of us. We can dismiss our healthcare system all we want, but I know the Lord works through systems. He helped me with financial provision throughout all three years of my business. I didn't pay more than $6 in those surgeries and urgent care visits, as I labored in love with the Lord in my fitness business.

The moral of the story is *He provides.* And He blesses others along the way. I very well could have never gone through either emergency room experience. Had I not, I wouldn't have had conversations with at least ten of the nurses and doctors around me. We never know how the Lord is encountering people's hearts around us or why He leads us on windy paths to find ourselves in certain rooms full of complete strangers. All I know is He turns bad situations for good by helping others along the way. My prayer is that the love of Jesus met my surgeon that day, or one of the nurses, or all of them. If even one person felt His love in the ER that day, it was worth it.

Daddy God takes care of us. He delights in the invitation to sit with us throughout the hospital gowns, preparation for surgery, and full journey to recovery, too. And as He holds our hand, He smiles at our steps of faith, even something as small as asking the nurse to push play to a worship song from an iPhone in the operating room.

CHAPTER 19

KINGDOM CAR

*H*ealthcare was important to me, but because I am my father's daughter, having a car was of the utmost importance. I know that sounds like I have my priorities backwards, but because I know my dad stresses over my safety and my need to get me from point "A" to point "B," I made it my priority to also pray that the Lord would provide a car for me. It was one of my biggest prayers at the time. I would say, "Papa, I will do whatever You ask with this business; please just take care of my car situation whenever mine dies."

My 2000 Honda was on its way out with over 200,000 miles of adventures on its wheels. Toward the end, there were a couple scares with the transmission. It provoked my dad and me to start car-hunting. I'm thankful I have an earthly father who is so helpful in the car department. Being in my late twenties, I probably should have been buying cars on my own, but at the time I hardly knew how to check my own oil. It's nice to have someone in your corner when making big decisions.

A good car guy is especially good to know. I had heard of a man named Scott from two different friends who recommended I reach out to him before looking anywhere else. They said he had fair prices and sold mostly Toyotas and Hondas. That got Dad's attention. Dad is a Honda guy to the very core. He always will be. Reliability and affordability are his two middle names.

The hunt was on. Every so often, we would drive to Scott's auto shop to search out the CRVs and RAV4s. I was praying for a black SUV, and I really liked the RAV4s, but every time Scott got one in, I would tell him, "Actually, my Honda seems to be running fine now." And every time we had a big scare with my car, Scott seemed to have just sold all of the RAV4s in my price range. We were "cars" passing in the night.

Thankfully, the Lord's timing is *perfect*. For two years, we all played this game of shop, hang on a little longer, search, and miss. It was all right though, because Scott loved sharing stories with us, and Dad and I loved hearing them. Car shopping at Scott's gave my dad and me something to do together, and quite honestly, I think it can be attributed to one of the reasons our relationship began to grow. Scott had a way of doing that. He had a fatherly approach to everything he did, and he did it all with a little touch of heaven. We could sense it, and it kept bringing us back.

When my Honda finally died, Scott mentioned using my car for parts, so we said our goodbyes to my college car as the tow truck man did his fancy hookups and drove away. Memories of dance parties between study sessions flashed before my eyes as we followed the tow truck into Scott's shop one last time. Per the usual, Scott welcomed us with open arms, but this time was different. I no longer had a car of my own for the drive home. I was officially car-less.

By this time, we were regulars. Not only that, but we were pretty good friends with Scott after sharing stories back and forth over the course of two years. He was a family man with a good memory and already knew every car desire in my heart. He showed us all he had on the lot at the time, knowing none of them fit my criteria. After our usual storytelling and catch-up session at Scott's desk, Dad grabbed for his keys to head home. That's when Scott gently asked, "Megan, you said you need a car, right?"

I knew it must have been a rhetorical question, but maybe it was similar to a prayer where Papa just wanted to hear me ask. I replied, "Yeah," in hopes he might have a new car coming in the next couple of days or weeks.

"Well, I have that ministry I told you about where I lend out cars to people. I just got one back. The driver's seat doesn't move, but we can test it out, and if it fits, you can have it for as long as you'd like."

And he meant it. He pulled around the corner with a beautiful 2003 white Acura. I had always wanted one, but in my practical mind and because I am a Prentice, I never even considered looking beyond the realm of Honda or Toyota. My best friend from college drove an Acura, and I always felt so classy in the passenger's seat. I never thought to ask Jesus for the *type* of car I wanted. My mind was set on all things practical. I guess the Lord knew. He's good like that. I did tell Him I wanted an SUV, white or black. He just filled in the gaps based on the desires in my heart. I tested out the seat, which was stuck in place on the farthest setting. It fit my long legs flawlessly. In fact, it appeared to be fit *just for me*. Sometimes with perfectly tailored gifts, I wonder if Jesus gets a little too much excitement out of our reactions.

Free car day was a fun surprise. We pulled up stressed and slightly expectant to buy a RAV4, which didn't happen. I left an hour later with the keys to a white Acura. It was "mine." Just like that. No exchange of money. *A free car*. I had that Acura for the next two years. I originally planned to buy a car during that time, but believe it or not, the one I was looking for never came. And Scott, never once, asked when I would return it. I guess Papa God whispered to his heart that I needed it.

I learned a lot about the Father's heart through Scott. Once, after a long twelve-hour day at the studio, I was so exhausted by nightfall that I backed out of a parking space and side-swiped a light post. I'm talking the *big* ones that light the entire parking lot with the concrete base. It left a dent. Or two. Actually, it left a full line across the back passenger door. I felt extreme fear and shame flood the car as I envisioned the conversation with Scott.

I texted him immediately the next day, in dread. I should have called, but I was so ashamed, and we were on a mostly-texting basis anyway, so I justified the informal communication. It's amazing how shame can instantly cripple us. I know now that shame is never from the Lord. Scott helped me to understand that as he replied with a simple, "It's okay. No big deal. Matthew 6:26."

I looked up the scripture he sent and cried. It talks about how birds don't sow or reap, and yet the Father still feeds them, and how we are of much greater value than the birds. I was in utter shock! Scott had already paid a parking ticket for me earlier that year for not having a front plate in a bougie part of town, *and now this*? How could I experience greater love than this? How could I experience greater mercy? I felt like I kept messing up and owed him so much for lending me a free car, and yet he kept pressing into my mistakes with relentless love. He *showed* me what grace really feels like. It's one thing to read the word on a page. It's another to experience it.

"Things" seem a lot less important, and people seem much more important when you look at everything as being borrowed, like that "free" white Acura. My perspective has shifted, many thanks to Jesus and Scott. Things are temporary. And so is this life. I love how Papa God provides material things *and* it always seems to come with a little life lesson, too. He's teaching me to dance in the rain and to dream in the storm, even when odds are against me. God beats out even the strongest odds. He provides in the wildest, most unexpected ways. I think that's His specialty so we know *He's the one* working everything out.

*Returning "my" white Acura to Scott after two
years with these hot wheels.*

TRAIT VIII

OUR CONSOLING FRIEND

CHAPTER 20

THE GIFT OF GROCERIES

*N*ot having a lot allowed the Lord to show His faithfulness in every area of my life. While owning my business and only making $12,500 a year, I somehow still had money in the bank. Even in looking at my spreadsheets, the budgeting didn't make sense. Only He could have made that happen. The Lord had provided a car and healthcare, and by attending my new church home, I found out about a food pantry every Sunday, so I also had free food. I used to have a stigma about people who received pantry food. In fact, I never did tell people where I was getting my food from, but for two full years, the Lord gave in abundance through donated items from Whole Foods and Sprouts. It wasn't always the freshest food in the pantry, but it was typically no worse than close-to-date food that shoppers were buying straight off the shelves in the grocery stores. The only difference was I would wait in line after church for my groceries, which ended up being a more convenient one-stop-shop on Sundays anyway.

After I humbled myself and got over the stigma of being a food pantry recipient, I started to ask the Lord for very random things. He romanced my heart weekly. In the days leading up to church, I would voice to my roommates, "Gosh, I really wish they had ginger tea at the pantry." The next day, I would show up, and there it would be. Not just any kind of tea, but ginger tea. And spicy, too. Just the way I liked it! God saw me. He cared. Even about something as small as bananas or frozen mangoes for my morning smoothies.

My groceries were the gifts that kept on giving. For those two years, I prayed and prayed for certain foods, and almost every week, I would get many of the specific items I had asked for. They were typically my favorite flavor or kinds, too. Not always, but I can tell you when I was craving butternut squash soup, there would be a butternut squash, green apple, onion, and carrots—all the fixings I needed for the most scrumptious soup on a snowy winter day!

I don't know this for sure, but I think the reason it was important for me to know it was the Lord giving through the pantry rather than "happenstance" was for my next hard season of life. If I had to guess, He timed His gifts just right in this tough season to carry me through an even harder season to come. As we get to know the Lord's love and character, we can then grow in our understanding of Him and mature as well. Maturity gives us a solid foundation of faith with roots that go deep. Deep roots mean we cannot be pulled away from His love, no matter what storm comes our way.

I felt seen by Jesus, and because I repeatedly saw His blessings in my life in such intimate ways, I trusted Him. I mean I *really* trusted Him. I trusted Him in the small things, which allowed me to hold tight to Him before walking through the bigger battles. And because I trusted Him, I got to share my stories with others, and they began to trust Him, too. They began to see Jesus show up in their lives as He met them in the intimate desires of their hearts. Faith is a substance. It's like a fragrance that starts as a liquid and becomes a perfume others can smell. And just as perfume can be spread through a hug, faith can be spread through story.

Another fun result of faith is favor. A friend once told me, "Favor is meant to be shared." Favor is another word for blessings that come your way, or "generosity from heaven." It wasn't until I started to share my pantry stories and collected additional carrots and onions for my roommates that I truly understood the heart of the Father. By giving to others and also sharing about my weekly miracles, it grew their faith, too.

It's like this: I was in the grocery store in Hawaii during the pandemic, and I had misplaced my credit card and ID. I had that sinking feeling of "someone must've stolen it." Then, I remembered not to blame others and figured I probably misplaced it. The next thought that followed was, *Shoot, I can't buy these groceries now.* I looked down, and thankfully I had a $20 bill stashed in the side of another pouch, but I knew the total would be close if not more. The man in front of me lingered for a bit as I checked out. The total rang in at $20.74. The man quickly handed the cashier a twenty in addition to my twenty. Though I only owed an additional $0.74, his act of kindness made me feel seen and loved. He said the common words we've heard before as I thanked him for his kindness, "You're welcome. Pay it forward."

I knew in that moment the Lord was confirming a thought I had been pondering all week: Faith is a substance and can be caught and shared. If faith can be shared, it must be something that can be widely spread, meaning we can actually "faith it forward" to someone else. Just like the man getting out his twenty to pay it forward, we can share our wild faith stories that can spur on a lethal faith for others—the kind of dangerous faith that can take out the enemy and his schemes. *If only we shared our stories of His faithfulness.*

That's the purpose of every word in this book. It's not some positive thinking that's dependent upon my own thoughts. It's real. Yes, there are hardships in life, and no, God doesn't answer every prayer of mine the way I expect or want Him to at times. But I do know that, in certain seasons of life and when I am aligned with His plan, He will show up and show off, and not just a little, but a whole lot. He provides in abundance to make His name known and to glorify Himself. Ultimately, that's what it's all about: knowing Him, walking with Him in the day-to-day and showing others what an adventure of a lifetime it is to do life with Jesus, no matter the circumstances. He makes everything better because He is the main target. *He is the end goal,* and we get changed in the process of following Him.

There was a time when I would share my story about the Guatemala trip and how I made the plane but the family that stayed behind to make room for me on the plane *did not.* Because I was so fresh in my walk with Jesus, still very self-focused, and riding the wave of His love for adventure, that family never even crossed my mind. It wasn't until someone pointed out the other side of the story that I realized my glory story with Jesus was someone else's longer road home. The Lord cared enough to romance my heart in that moment, and He also showed me that seasons change, and hopefully our hearts grow to be more like Jesus if we are following Him.

In the next big season of life, after my plane adventures, Jesus showed me the beauty of missing a flight to have church on an airport floor. He simply needed me to step out in faith and share what was on His heart with my new friend in need of a touch from Him. He showed me it was best to throw out my agenda, to skip class at my studio, and to encourage His son toward the dreams in his heart.

Sometimes I get caught up in previous seasons of life and the ways God worked "before," and I forget to seek Him in the here and now. He's in the present. He's ever creating, meaning we won't always get to see Him in the same ways we used to, and though it might be different now, if we are open to it, we just might like the new chapter with Him even better than the previous one.

I don't know the other side of the story for that trip in the Honolulu airport. Maybe the standby passenger who got that last seat experienced the goodness of God for the first time. I do know God works everything together for the good of those who love Him. That means *all* who truly love and desire life with Him. Every person. Every circumstance. Every plane ride. Every hospital visit. Every grocery store trip. I like to look for Him and what He is doing in each moment and season of life. He is in the details. And He makes everything more beautiful.

CHAPTER 21

FLOWERS FROM HEAVEN

*B*eauty is God's middle name. Look at the ocean and the abundance of colors in the coral reefs or the spectrum of bright fruit ranging from yellows to oranges to purples. My best friend from college always said she knows there's a God because of fruit. I agree. What a tasty gift of sweetness after a savory meal.

As I've grown older, flowers have become one of my favorite forms of beauty. I used to think they were a waste of time and money because they would look great for a day or two, maybe five tops, and then die. It was too much work to change the water and replace the darn things every week, and all for a price. They were beautiful, but a little too high maintenance for an efficient minimalist like me.

It wasn't until "pantry season" that God changed my mind about flowers. When the leftover flowers from Sprouts showed up every week at church, I found myself growing to love the pops of color in the corner of my bedroom, next to my Jesus-ladder. It was a tossup between Jesus and my boyfriend at the time for who was more generous in the flower-giving department. Let's just say I felt like one lucky gal. (By the way, ladies, every single one of you deserves "just because" flowers. If you haven't gotten any, maybe it's time to ask!)

The first few weeks, I would get every kind of white flower imaginable. I loved that it matched the theme of my room. Then, I started to explore new options of multi-colored bouquets and red roses. The fact that I can even write this right now still has me in awe of the Lord and His kindness.

About 25 bouquets later and toward the end of a rocky relationship, I needed to get away and decided, "Why not jet to Australia for a long weekend?" Yes, you heard me. I flew nineteen hours straight with a full twenty-hour time difference for a 3-day, 4-night weekend with a friend north of Sydney. I knew things with my boyfriend weren't going well and the beach was always my healing spot. My boyfriend and I had decided to fast ten full days from communication with one another to seek guidance from the Lord.

As you already know, when I commit to something, I commit big. It sounds crazy, but on my nineteen hour flight to Australia, I actually ran out of quality time with the Lord. My type-A personality had set aside four hours for Bible reading, six hours for sleeping, two hours for Bible study, another couple of hours for stretch breaks, worship, take off and meals, and five remaining hours for finishing the book I was reading, *When Heaven Invades Earth*. Not only did I finish my book on the way over, but I read the whole book of Romans, too. I was glued.

When we got the announcement for landing, I can clearly remember thinking to the Lord, *Wow, that was fast.* Who can say that about a flight to Australia? I guess time really does go quickly when you're having fun! Although, fun isn't necessarily the word I would use since I knew I was on the verge of a breakup with my boyfriend. He was across the world doing work in Puerto Rico, and I was now in Australia. At least we both had the beach.

The last day of the trip, my friend went off to have "her time" while I stayed behind to journal. I decided that day, mostly because of the book I had just finished, love truly was a choice, and I needed to either choose my boyfriend or not. I decided for the first time in my life to choose him, regardless of if he chose me. After all, that's what Jesus did. That's real love, choosing someone and loving them, even if they might not choose you or love you back. I spent an entire hour writing out a letter, telling him the conclusion I had come to after seeking the Lord. I prayed and prayed that God would speak to his heart, too, and that God would lead us to the same conclusion. I also prayed that, if we weren't the best mates for one another, the Lord would lead us apart.

We broke our communication "fast" through a premature Facetime call to coordinate time-sensitive decisions. When he answered, his voice was not his happy, light-hearted tone. It was short and a little cold. The sting was piercing. I knew in those first two seconds of talking that it was over. All of it. Over.

I didn't understand.

"Daddy God, why would You have me come to this conclusion of choosing him if he wouldn't choose me back? I asked You to bring us both to the same conclusion."

I couldn't take another heartbreak. I'd had one too many between the doors closing twice to Africa, the numerous and continuous letdowns of the studio, and prior relationship turmoil. It was too much to bear.

And then I heard the still small voice of God, "You love because I first loved you."

The flight home wasn't quite the same as the flight out. It was filled with a lot of tears and sleep. My heart felt like it had been wrung out, and I'm sure the person next to me on the flight could feel it. I wasn't hungry, and everywhere I went for the three days after I landed, I listened to worship. I carried my phone around like a little "boombox" (throwback to my fellow 90s kids). And as I carried my phone, the Lord carried my heart. Being with the Lord wasn't an option. I *needed* Him. I didn't merely want Him. I needed Him to survive. Or at least I felt like it.

I'm amazed how strong the emotion of love can be. It really is wild. You hear of people dying of broken hearts. It makes sense when you look at it from a heavenly perspective and how the Lord wired us to love so deeply. I understand when people say that now. I've never felt the heavy, thick, weighty love of God so much as I did during those three days. I didn't do much else except worship, read about Him, and fall into His arms as my loving Comforter. He was better than any chocolate, ice cream, or chick flick. I asked Him to hold my heart and to truly heal it. And He did. Not right away, *but He really did.*

Not everything has to be a lesson in life. It can take the joy, peace, or comfort out of life to be too analytical all the time. I know a lot of us like to "get in our head" and to "figure God out" in our circumstances. Sometimes it's just good to be childlike and "be," but we already read that chapter.

In this instance, though, I did have one breakthrough lesson that I clung to. I've heard it over and over before, but it wasn't until I walked through it myself that I realized *love is a choice.* It wasn't until I walked through choosing someone who didn't choose me back that I realized the pain Jesus experiences daily with many of us who don't choose Him. I felt the heart of God on the deepest level I had known, and it broke me to know that

Jesus has that same deep love for us even when we don't choose Him back, or when we have chosen Him but we don't choose Him *first*. I often chose unhealthy amounts of work hours over spending time with Him. I chose to daydream about food or marriage or my next big step in life over Him. I even chose small and stupid things like scrolling through social media for countless hours over being with Him.

That deep sorrow led me into a long season of "me and Jesus." I asked Him to protect my heart and to shield me from any men until my season of marriage. It lasted over three years. It's a scary prayer to pray, but even scarier was the pain I felt when He revealed the hurt of not choosing the greatest Lover of my soul daily. I can honestly say I didn't even "see" men romantically for those three years, which was really saying something for a gal who used to tirelessly scan every room I entered looking for my future soulmate.

The Sunday after returning from Australia was day three of the breakup. I was late to church and had been praying for my favorite bright yellow flowers, sunflowers. Most of the donated flowers were gone if I didn't arrive early enough, but my heart was too tired to care to get to church on time. People would scavenge the flowers early and take flowers to their seats, so there wasn't a lot of hope any were left. Yet, I prayed anyway. When I arrived fifteen minutes late to church, I turned the corner to a table *full* of flowers. They weren't just any flowers. The table looked like a meadow of *sunflowers*! The sunflowers were staring back at me, bright and beautiful, as if Jesus were saying, "You want sunflowers? I will give you the whole store!" That was a first. They typically would have been picked over, but I had an abundance to choose from. I guess it makes sense because Jesus is a God of plenty with access to all the riches and the most beautiful flowers of all. To say I felt seen and loved is an understatement.

I returned home to replace my brown and decaying flowers my ex had sent weeks earlier with my bright new sunflowers. The Lord knew I didn't need any reminders of the hard road I was walking. He brought me new and beautiful memories with Him, instead.

The next week, I didn't ask for flowers because my others were still blooming somewhat strong. Yet, when I arrived at church, this time, I found not only more sunflowers, but white roses, too! I went home with two bouquets that day and felt the Lord say, "Take them both. I have an abundance, and you are worth more than one."

I love white roses. They matched my simple room decor and white color-scheme, which the Lord reminded me signifies purity and cleansing. There is a time to share favor and a time to receive. This mourning process was a time to receive. I've learned over the years, too, that having a heart to receive can often be more difficult than giving. Sometimes we rob people *and* the Lord of the joy of giving when we can't freely receive.

Jesus doesn't toy with our hearts. I used to think He did with each consecutive loss I endured. It may feel like it for a season, but anytime we *feel* that way we need to go back to truth, *the* Truth. He already gave everything to be with us. He wants to hold our hearts, not toy with them. And when our feelings don't align with that truth, we need to keep coming back to it until we believe it. We need to remember His love. And if we don't have love stories of our own with Him, that's what friends are for. That's what faith stories are for. That's why we get to "faith it forward."

The flower miracles continued for a year. And the flowers were wonderful to receive, especially in a time of mourning, but ultimately, the flowers and gifts weren't the point. He is. He already proved His love when He crawled up on a cross to experience the greatest pain so we can have the greatest gift of all: Him. That statement He made by continuing forward to the cross, despite sweating blood, was the greatest statement of love He could have ever made. Jesus doesn't make questionable statements. He makes ones that offend every fiber of our beings because, despite the unfathomable pain and emotional rejection, *He chose us*. And He continues to choose us daily. We can have confidence in knowing exactly where He stands and how He feels about us. He wears His heart on His sleeve. Whether we accept it or not is *our choice*.

*Strolling back from the beach while attempting to
surf during my four-day vacation to Australia.*

TRAIT IX

UNDERPAID & OVERQUALIFIED LIFE COACH

CHAPTER 22

BREAKING CHAINS

*I*t's funny how we can go into a God-appointed situation with an agenda when the Lord has something entirely different in mind. Toward the beginning of my faith walk, before I had a church community, I started to dabble in attending a smaller church with an acquaintance. I still popped in and out of the larger megachurches where I could easily get lost and felt like a number. Yet, I felt a magnetic draw to attend the smaller church every so often.

I quickly found a tight-knit group of friends my age at the smaller church. They deeply loved Jesus and had a hunger to know Him more. I found myself learning a lot from them and encountering the Lord even more by being with them. Who would have thought I could encounter the Lord *with* other people? What a concept! I had gotten so used to worshipping alone in the corner that this was a welcomed change.

As I grew into my new group of friends, I started to attend their Thursday night weekly dinners. It easily became my favorite night of the week. I found myself getting excited whenever Wednesday rolled around because it meant Thursday was coming. I always left recharged, full, and joyful. That's why when I heard the news that my high school track buddy had passed away from a battle with cancer, I didn't feel like talking and definitely didn't feel like sharing the devastating news with my newfound friends. It felt too heavy to bring to others, and I didn't have capacity to "go there." Satan loves to lie to us about community when we need people most. He makes it seem like the better plan is to retreat and hide the burden from others when the reality is we *need* others. When one of us is weak, another is strong. We were created to hold each other's arms up in the battle and fight *for* our comrades. It's the beauty of doing life *together*.

After some prodding and poking from a friend, I reluctantly drove over to our Thursday night group, but I made it clear it was *only* to pray for my friend's family. When I walked in the door, I knew I had made the right choice. It was the same laid-back ambiance as always, and there was no need to "perform." We were ourselves, and there was freedom to just "be." Be sad. Be heard. Be silent.

Finding a community where you can "just be" is a treasure. It is still one of my favorite community group memories to this day. It felt so safe. And though we were all different, we passionately loved Jesus and wanted to learn and know Him more. We did whatever, whenever to *know Him*. We often worshipped with a talented guitar player named Johnny. Every time he picked up a guitar, God's tangible love and thick Presence would blanket the room, any room. Johnny carried the heart of God wherever he went, and it was powerful to experience.

As we gathered to pray on that somber Thursday, I shared about my friend's lost battle to cancer and asked for prayer for his family. The prayer was powerful, yet I was tired. I got up to leave, and I heard Johnny, the worship leader, say, "Wait, I feel like there's something else God wants to do." I highly respected

Johnny. He was the closest representation of Jesus I had experienced. When he spoke, I listened. So, I stuck around.

Johnny picked up his guitar and began to sing. I felt the Lord tugging on my heart to give in to the tears of pain and confusion. With the tears came an annoying hope as I felt the Lord also nudging me to let go of the disappointment of my friend not getting healed. As I opened my heart, other doors in my heart began to crack open. I was carrying a heaviness of trying to please my parents after being jobless and living in their basement. I wasn't sure how this related to my friend and praying for his family, but it mattered to God, and it was surfacing.

As Johnny sang one last song, I crawled to the floor, face down as the weight of everything I was carrying let loose. With every "Break every chain" chorus that Johnny sang, wild sobs and snot bubbles found their way out of my body. I felt as though I were undergoing heart surgery while running a marathon all at once. It was painful in the best way possible. There's no other way to describe it. The pain was leaving, and the snot-crying on the floor was embarrassing in front of my new friends, but I didn't feel like I could stop it, nor did I care. Healing was happening, and it was happening fast. It felt like a forceful wind had swept through and left, and all during one song.

And then, I felt the "high" you get from running and the healing touch you experience after a deep tissue massage, all wrapped up in one moment and one song. You know when you have a good cry and let everything out? It was like that but a hundred times better. I was lighter. My actual body felt as if I weighed less.

I knew this Thursday was no longer about my friend and his family. I walked in heavy. *I left free.* I didn't even know the weight of what I was carrying until it was gone. No more parent-pleasing to be done. God was dismantling every chain I had ever picked up and shackled around my own wrists. Every test, every cooked meal, every art project, every soccer game, every job, every area where I felt I had fallen short. And all in one moment, *I was enough.* Just me. I could feel the tangible hug of God as I felt Him impress upon my heart, "You are enough, Megan." And I *believed* Him. *I was enough.*

I was enough for Jesus, and that was all that mattered. I never did go back to that lie. I was marked forever that night. People *are* still being healed in an instant. We see it all the time in the Bible. And it still happens today. Maybe all Jesus is waiting on is your *yes*. *Yes* to Him. *Yes* to freedom. *Yes* to *believing* Him and leaving the false comforts of pain behind.

CHAPTER 23

SILENCING FEAR

*M*y voice used to terrify me. I had near-panic attacks almost every time I raised my hand to speak in class, and it was typically because I *had* to in order to get a participation grade. Somewhere along the way, I started believing my voice wasn't worth being heard, and I responded by either demanding attention in the room or by sinking back into the corner and watching others interact in the present moment. One was a cover-up. The other was fear.

Fear can be crippling. And once I started to care about what others thought of me, it only added to the already-excruciating anxiety of speaking aloud. The worst part of fear is it breeds more fear. The longer we cling to it, the more paralyzing it can become. The longer I told myself public speaking wasn't for me, the more I embodied that mentality—and it didn't seem any speech class was going to change that. I felt too far-gone.

As I made my way into college, the paralyzing fear of public speaking grew into a fear of singing in front of others, reading aloud, and even telling stories in small groups of people. If I had to give it a name, anxiety would probably be the most fitting word, though I didn't know it at the time.

Graduating into adulthood presented some challenges when I found myself in roles of community outreach and sales. I had to give presentations, which meant *public speaking*. I learned tricks of the trade from CEOs and renowned leaders in my office jobs, yet the fear still gripped me every time I had to masquerade in front of more than five people.

I continuously pleaded with the Lord to break my fear and make me an eloquent speaker. I knew, if He could do it for Moses, He could most certainly do it for me, too. The nonprofit job seemed to boost my confidence a bit more, as I found myself giving daily tours to mid-sized groups of all ages. I partnered with the Girl Scout troops all across Denver and then throughout the nation, too. If I had a *thin mint* for every tour I gave, I'd probably be a very large gal. The tours eased my comfort level a bit, but they still didn't seem to sever the fear.

One ordinary day, I received a phone call from a woman at church. I respected her as the powerhouse woman she was and because we ran in the same circles, we decided to finally connect. She was planning for a women's conference, and I had a list of at least five people for her to meet. From one fellow connector to another, our dreaming brains started to flow. As the call progressed, it seemed I had more in common with this woman than I thought. Our conversation turned into a spontaneous interview, and before I hung up, I had somehow committed to praying about speaking at the holistic health conference.

As with many other events in my life, I didn't think I would actually step forward and commit. I figured the "I'll pray about it and see what the Lord says" would be a *no* and I'd continue on my comfortable path. Yet, when I felt a peace and healthy fear from the Lord to continue as one of the featured speakers at the conference, I committed wholeheartedly.

I was in my late twenties and had never taken any sort of public speaking classes or seminars. I love how the Lord qualifies the unqualified, though. This powerhouse woman later became my mentor and friend, and because *she* believed in me, I started to believe in myself. I started to trust the Lord in *both* of us, and it gave me the courage I needed to step forward.

I thought about the conference every single day leading up to the moment I took the microphone on that platform. It wasn't always a healthy fear either. But, something in me believed that if the Lord, with whom I had already created so much history, believed I could do it, *then I could do it*. Who was I to say otherwise?

The conference began, women gathered and worshipped, and my mind started to wander down a nervous trail. Then, the final opening speaker took the stage. She was a fierce and no-nonsense, ex-military woman dressed in camo. As I began to internalize all of the ways I could mess up, I felt as if our sergeant was calling me out in front of the whole room as she addressed my exact thoughts: "It's not about you. None of it is. We do it because God told us to."

For some reason, it was the wake-up call I needed. *Speaking wasn't about me.* The message the Lord put in me was to be shared and released. The faith stories aren't tangible if not shared. And so, I committed *scared, yet willing*.

The morning of, I awoke at three wide-eyed and nervous. I replayed the scripted bullet points I had rehearsed so many times over and over in my head. The nervous thoughts started to circle. *I am speaking today . . . at a conference. Me. I never thought I would speak to a large group. Ever.*

It didn't help the nerves when I found out I was scheduled to speak in the afternoon. That was just enough time to talk myself out of it. Yet, the sergeant's voice kept running through my head: *It's not about you. It's not about you.*

Ultimately, her tough love got me up on stage. And you know what? The Holy Spirit showed up big time. He blanketed the entire room and even brought some passionate tears to my eyes. *Because it wasn't about me.* It was about the women sitting in front of me. The Lord knew they needed the message He put in me, and He gave me the nudge I needed to step onto the platform and conquer my greatest fear of all time.

I did it, and I did it afraid. But, I wasn't alone that day. It's hard to explain when people say, "The Lord spoke through me," but He did. Even my mentor walked by and said she could tangibly feel the thick Presence of God from outside the room. I am thankful for fierce women of God who see the gold in us. And I never thought I would say this, but I am thankful for drill sergeants who push us to our limits. Sometimes we need a little "kick in the pants" to get us out of our small "me world." And sometimes when we hear the lies saying, "You're going to fail," we just need a really big God shouting louder, "You've got this!" They say you become like the five closest people around you. Surround yourself with mentors, drill sergeants, and the greatest Life Coach of all time, and fear won't stand a chance.

Standing onstage and conquering my biggest fear
of speaking at the 2018 women's "Whole and
Free" conference in Denver.

TRAIT X

MINISTRY MENTOR

CHAPTER 24

GAS STATION CHURCH

*S*ometimes I get on these health kicks where I enjoy making weird creations that are a healthier version of the original. I was invited to my friend's for dessert and a fire, and she liked healthy food, too, so I attempted my dairy-free brownies, complete with black beans instead of eggs and milk. Extra protein. Healthy and yummy.

I was running late because the brownies took a bit longer than planned. Actually, let's be honest, they were a last-minute addition as I was running out the door, so I was already twenty-five minutes late. I've gotten better about my punctuality since then.

On the drive over, I was passing a gas station that had the cheapest gas in town. My thrifty self *had* to pull over to fill my tank. *I was already late, why not another ten minutes?* I reasoned. I shot my friend another "I'm going to be a bit longer" apology text. As I pulled out of the gas station, I saw a homeless man with a sign. I always want to help, but don't often know what to say, so I pulled away. I turned right at the light, and as I turned, I felt the Lord nudge me to circle back. I couldn't deny it. After a long debate with myself, I pulled back into the gas station and decided that most people like brownies and a lot also like black beans, so at the very least, I figured I could offer him a couple of brownies.

Not knowing what else to say, I pulled up and said, "Hi! Would you like a brownie? I experimented with black beans, so I can't promise they are good, but you're welcome to them." He took two, probably just to make me feel good about my new creation. I appreciated his efforts to do so.

I don't normally ask strangers into my car unless I get a strong impression from the Lord to extend the invitation. It's only been three times in my life since I am a single gal. This was one of those times. I asked if he wanted to come inside, and he said *yes*. Then, I asked about his day, and he started to tell me his whole life story which turned into a conversation about planets and space and a lot of stuff that was way over my head. He said he used to be a scientist of some kind, and I smiled and nodded as he continued to educate me on things I haven't studied since fourth grade. Then, he pointed to the scar running from one ear to the middle of his forehead, and he said, "I used to do all of that until I got this. I was in a really bad car accident and was launched from my vehicle across the highway." He continued to tell me his brain didn't function the way it used to.

I asked if I could pray for his head, and he graciously accepted and told me he knew God but wanted to know Him more and didn't know how. I asked if he knew Jesus. He said he did but he had never talked to Him before. I asked if he wanted to talk to Jesus and have a relationship with Him so that he could continue to talk to Jesus whenever he wanted. The man's joy and excitement were so contagious that it ignited passion deep within me and I began to pray boldly.

It was my first time praying the "salvation prayer" with some- one, and it was quite an interesting one. The Holy Spirit led me into talking about how He created the planets and galaxies and how He knew this gentleman intimately. It was completely tailored to this man's heart. He repeated after me as he accepted Jesus for the first time. He thanked me profusely, and I started to tear up as I drove off, reminding him that he could now talk with Jesus whenever he wanted about whatever he wanted.

I almost didn't stop that day. I was in the rush of life, making vegan brownies for social activities with friends. I was getting last-minute gas at a gas station. But Jesus had another plan. He wanted to have a small church service to the left of the gas pump with his son who was hungry to know Him but didn't know where to start. The seeds in the man's heart were already cultivated. They just needed a little watering by someone who had the time to stop. We can so easily miss the Lord's little invitations if we are caught up in the "go-go-go" of life. We often talk about revival in our church and world. This is it. Revival looks like Jesus spontaneously flagging us down to have black bean brownies with his son at a gas station.

CHAPTER 25

TOILET SEAT ENCOUNTERS

I've always found the best leaders to be the humblest ones. Look at Moses. He was known as the humblest man in the world, and though he needed a little confidence booster from the Lord to walk his path, he led millions of Israelites to the Promised Land. Humble leaders typically have the most influence, but you would never know it because they don't talk about it. They know who they are, and therefore, they don't need to boast about what they've done. My friends in Uganda who started the best-ranked school and partnered with local Ugandans to start businesses, hospitals, and community programs have completely transformed an entire village and beyond, but you would never know it if you sat across the table from them.

I admire humble people. Jesus tops the charts. The problem is I have really needed help in the humility department. I grew up feeling the need to prove myself in whatever I did because I thought that performance and "doing" was who I was. The Lord taught me to unlearn those thoughts and, in the words of my friend, to "deconstruct" all the lies. It almost seems more difficult to unlearn our wrong thoughts and habits than to learn entirely new ones.

Pride is gross. If we are honest with ourselves, I think any of us would agree. When someone boasts of their achievements, it makes me squirm inside, and probably on the outside, too. That's why, when I operate in pride, the apostle Paul's words resonate to my very core, "For what I want to do I do not do, but what I hate I do" (Romans 7:15b). It's not that I want to be prideful; it simply comes out of me because it hasn't quite been worked out of me yet.

Humility lessons with the Lord are sometimes the hardest, but they are the absolute most fruitful. I couldn't ask for a more powerful lesson in transformation. Ultimately, that's our goal, isn't it? To become more like Jesus? To become love and truth and peace and joy? Humility is the quickest way to get there, but that's a catch-22 because humility is not a "fast track" for most of the people I've met, and it hasn't been for me either.

After shutting down my fitness business, I wanted to dream with the Lord about what was next. The hard part was *I couldn't dream*. Everything I had envisioned my future to be involved fitness franchises, instructor curriculums, and a holistic wellness space, including several other wellness practices. Every time I tried to re-envision my future, I was led back to the same idea and with it, came a sick feeling in the pit of my stomach and what felt like the weight of a hundred elephants. It felt heavy, raw, and unhealed. I even tried to step back into instructing by helping to teach a trial class for a studio in south Denver. There was no grace. I was scatterbrained and fumbled through my words the entire time. I think the ladies felt badly for me. The Lord shut it down before I could even get into a rhythm. Thank goodness. I praise Him for closed doors that lead me away from wild goose chases!

I was left still questioning, "What's next?" I continued in some modeling jobs, and I was getting occasional dog sitting jobs, but I felt the Lord preparing me for a move. I knew that meant I needed to start saving. Typically, in the past, I went ahead of the Lord's timing, and He had to slow my roll. So, this time around, I decided to wait on Him, no matter how long it took. Yet, it seemed He was taking forever. I waited and waited and waited some more. I wasn't getting any feedback when I prayed, so I asked the Lord to forgive me if I had overlooked anything.

We are told to pray without ceasing, so that's exactly what I did. And as I prayed, I started having faint flashbacks to high school when some of the other cheerleaders on my team cleaned houses for a side job. I had always felt a little "above" cleaning houses. After all, I got a 4.0 in high school and worked my tail off in college to get a four-year degree. Surely the Lord wouldn't call me to *that*. Yet, the thought kept returning. It wasn't until I had a conversation with one of my former roommates who said she started working with a cleaning company as a side gig that I felt the deep pit in my stomach urging me forward. It was a good and needed prodding. Kind of like a slap in the face to shake the pride off that had been lingering for over thirteen years.

I still, in the depths of my prideful heart, wasn't entirely sure if the Lord was calling me to clean houses. I did what we do when we don't want to follow what Jesus is calling us to do: I kept praying. Because I had already been walking through a wildly humbling season already, I figured it was time to be pulled out of the pit, and up the mountain with Him. I thought He was going to elevate me for my faithfulness, especially because so many people were speaking those things over me. It's not that I was being disobedient because, as my friends would tell you, I truly have a heart to obey the Lord. I guess it wasn't *crystal clear* so I figured more prayer couldn't hurt.

One Sunday, I was called onstage in front of the entire church, and a well-renowned speaker started to prophesy some things over my life. It hit me so hard that I crumbled on the floor as my spirit longed for the things he was saying to come true. I sobbed for hours until I had no strength left. When I got home from that experience and after a coffee date with my pastor and his wife, I figured maybe I should ask that speaker if he needed any help. I felt the Lord telling me to "apprentice" in that season of life, so why not ask? After all, we are told, "We do not have because we do not ask" (James 4:2).

I wrote the speaker a short and to-the-point email, and he responded with his number. I called him immediately on my way home from a counseling appointment. He seemed quite interested—until he wasn't. We had brainstormed ideas about me apprenticing under him and traveling the world. It seemed great and exciting after the last ten years of hardship I had walked through with career and business failures. I needed a "win."

But this wasn't it. I never heard back from him. Not even a reply. I did pray for a closed door if the opportunity wasn't from the Lord. The thing about bold prayers is the Lord actually listens and answers *very* clearly.

I went back to the drawing board with the Lord. In my conversation with the speaker, I remembered saying, "I will do anything you need. I'll scrub toilets if I have to!"

The Lord had me linger over those words. They felt significant. I almost felt my heart cringe as He impressed upon me, *If you will scrub toilets for a well-renowned speaker with a platform, will you scrub toilets for Me?*

That was it. To toilet-cleaning I went. I called up my old roommate's boss to see if he had work for me. Sure enough, he did. I started that Monday. I think I called him on a Friday. I guess Jesus was eager to get me into the toilet-scrubbing business! After all, I was thirteen years overdue. That's the thing about growing with Jesus. If He wants you to learn something, you can't escape it. He will keep on tapping and nudging until you give in, even if it takes thirteen years.

The first day was a learning day. It was very enlightening to observe how you clean from top-to-bottom and use certain products on certain surfaces. I have to say, I enjoyed it! The second day was even better because I was "released" from supervision and got to listen to podcasts and worship music. Over the course of the next two months, I began to really enjoy cleaning. In fact, it was one of my favorite jobs yet because I didn't feel like I had anyone to disappoint, and after being a big-time visionary for so long and not getting to see my dreams actualize, it was fulfilling to walk into a space and see a complete transformation within two hours.

I only got to clean my favorite house twice, but both times made enough of an impact to change me forever. I walked up the spiral wooden staircase to a long hardwood floor corridor that looked like it could be the replica of a newly remodeled *Titanic*. It was a brand-new home that smelled of fresh wood and tile. Everything looked untouched, and quite honestly, I probably could have eaten off the floor of the master bath because it was so shiny and clean *before* I even got there. I worked my way upstairs, but it wasn't until I went to the middle-school daughter's bathroom that I started to weep.

As I listened to worship music, I got into the shower (my least favorite area to clean). I decided to embrace the task and with that, the season I was in. I didn't understand it, but I wasn't going to fight it, either. As I scrubbed, I saw a piece of paper that read,

Things to Do:

1. Take a Shower
2. Put on lotion
3. Go to [my sister's] room and braid her hair

I stopped reading there. I couldn't go on. I felt the Presence of God flood me and overwhelm me with His love for these girls and the love they had for one another. These were middle-schoolers! I was not making goals to braid my sister's hair when I was that age. I had a lot more important things on the agenda like passing notes between lockers on the way to class and planning who to sit with on the weekend bus rides to snow-board Copper Mountain.

When I got to the second sister's bathroom, she too had a list of goals. She was the older sister, and I was *just* as blessed by her list. As I worked my way over to her shower, the Presence of God was so thick I couldn't stand. I had to squat down as I sprayed and scrubbed the alcohol-solution onto the white tile. I was so full of joy I couldn't hold it in any longer and I erupted into praise as tears filled my eyes in complete fulfillment.

A mixture of my fresh tears hit the alcohol solution on the floor, and I felt the warmth of the Holy Spirit flood my chest as I was reminded of Mary who had the honor of washing Jesus' feet with her tears. I cleaned high and low as ten minutes turned into thirty with only one task left: the toilet. As I was scrubbing, I felt Jesus smile and say, "I just want to be where you are." My eyes continued to well up with tears as I sang those words back to Him. It reminded me of our airport moments together where time stood still. I had nowhere else to be. If Jesus was scrubbing toilets, that's *exactly* where I wanted to be.

My typical cleaning schedule was two houses back-to-back. There was one occurrence where I got called from one house to go to another to help some girls finish the cleaning in time. I was relieved to jump in my car and take a break from the current house. I needed a refresher, and I think Jesus knew it. On the drive over, the Lord had really been stirring my heart to pray for the church to "wake up" and walk in the *boldness* and *power* He died on the cross to give us. To really see people walking in freedom.

In that same moment, I experienced a heavy feeling of depression sweep over me, and I knew it was an evil spirit hovering over that city. I wasn't having it. Windows down, I immediately cranked my worship music as I battled through the song in the spirit, "Way maker, miracle worker, promise keeper, light in the darkness, my God, that is who you are." I renounced all spirits of depression and asked the Lord to come and *do something*.

Right when I uttered those words, I saw a teenage boy all dressed in black, head down with black hair covering his eyes. He sulked and sauntered down the sidewalk. He was walking in the opposite direction from the house I was called to clean. I could *feel* the depression as he disappeared behind me. It's as if the enemy was portraying the physical representation of depression I was rebuking right there in front of me through this boy. It was taunting, as if the devil was saying he had won. I started to get heated and fired up, and I said, "Lord, do something about depression! Do something about anxiety. Do something about suicide! Please, please, just *do something!*"

Immediately, the lyrics from the Matthew West song that was written about my friends in Uganda popped into my head, and I felt the Lord respond very clearly saying, "I did. I created you. *You do something.*" It was easy for me to question the voice, but after what I had experienced at the gas station, I knew it was

Jesus, and I knew I needed to flip a U-turn. I did question the Lord once more and said, "Lord, I want to honor my boss because I am 'on the job' and getting paid for this drive time."

I felt as if He responded, again, very clearly, "I gave you this job."

I decided that was enough questioning, flipped around and pulled up next to this boy. What I hadn't prepared were the words to approach him. After asking if he was okay, he replied a little disgruntled, "Yeah, I'm just out for a walk."

I wasn't off to a good start. Then, I decided to ask if he needed a ride anywhere. He said, "Sure." He then told me that he could use a ride to get some "smokes" right down the road. He hopped in, and I immediately asked Jesus what to tell him.

Jesus said, "Tell him he is seen."

So, I did. I told him he was seen by Jesus.

The boy's demeanor shifted. His hunched shoulders straightened as he lifted his head, and his eyes grew twice their usual size as he nearly sang, "*I was just talking to Jesus!* Do you know Jesus?"

He proceeded to tell me how he was hearing voices in his head to hurt himself and asking Jesus to take them away. I asked if I could pray against the voices with him, and he accepted the prayer, openheartedly. We prayed, and then just like that, he thanked me and continued on his way.

As the door closed, I looked at my clock. The entire process of flipping a U-turn, picking him up, praying, and dropping him off took me all of six minutes. I timed it. I thought back to the gas station brownies and this moment and wondered what our world might be like if we stopped and asked to see things from God's perspective. Jesus tells me quite often that people are not an inconvenience, and I think that's been one of my favorite messages *because they aren't.*

I got so much joy from watching the Lord touch the heart of a boy who just wanted to be "seen." It was an honorable gift for me to be invited into seeing the boy's depression lift as he shifted into his true identity as a loved son. I don't know where he is today, but I believe that encounter tapped into deep places in his heart. That's my prayer anyway. I leave the rest up to Jesus. All I can do is listen, and when Jesus says, "Pull over," I pull over, even if I don't have the most eloquent introduction. Thank goodness all He needs is a willing heart and maybe a U-turn or two.

*Adventuring with one of the most humble women
I have ever known who inspired me to finally step
into cleaning houses during our days of living in
the women's community home.*

TRAIT XI
SOUL & RELATIONSHIP HEALER

CHAPTER 26

MALL MAKEOVER

*R*ejection is part of life. It's especially part of being a business owner. I learned that lesson the hard way right away. I thought everyone would follow through, and because my business was faith-based, I assumed that meant every faith-based organization in town would want to collaborate. Assumptions are setups for disappointment. One assumption after another led me to more and more disappointment. I was disappointed in myself. I was disappointed in people. I was disappointed in the Lord. All in all, my heart wasn't in a good place. As the Bible tells us, "Hope deferred makes the heart sick" (Proverbs 13:12). I was in the thick of heartsickness and only getting sicker, but my driver personality kept propelling me forward.

One of the organizations I wanted to collaborate with most was a newer Christian T-shirt line. I loved their product, and they had recently launched a store in the local mall. When the Lord told me to go to the mall one morning for my business marketing strategy for the day, my mind went off into "Never Neverland." I imagined us holding weekly classes in their store, and maybe even collaborating through a fitness line. I dreamt of how our partnership would be the perfect way to build both of our businesses. Apparently, the Lord had something else in mind that day.

I walked into the Christian store that morning with business cards, ready for an impromptu meeting. No one came. I couldn't be that upset, seeing as it wasn't a scheduled meeting. I figured I would try again later. Surely the Lord wanted us to collaborate as faith-based companies seeking to glorify Him. Over the course of the next two years, I tried to reach out and network on countless occasions. Frustration grew, and I finally surrendered the dream of ever working with the T-shirt company, knowing they were a larger brand and I was just a baby studio in need of friends and clients. My heart held on to yet another failure, and the heartsickness continued to spread.

Years passed, and the Lord started to chip away at my hardened heart. I remember praying very specifically that the Lord would *value* me in the business world. I surrendered, and I trusted Him, but after years of foregoing income with my business and living on donated food and transportation, I craved to *feel* like I was the royalty He promised I was. Yet again, I was surprised by His response.

As I slaved away in my business, I found myself connecting with people and missions in all kinds of industries. Connectors tend to be friends with other connectors, so I often met people with one degree of separation to me, though still they were new faces. This was one of those times and I got to meet a friend of a friend and learn about his concept of turning encouraging phrases and scriptures into temporary tattoos! Seeing as I hadn't had a temporary tattoo since my playground days, I was quite intrigued and getting a tattoo was long over-due. I loved the idea of incorporating the scripture tattoos into my fitness classes. Over my cup of chai, I explained how I could use the tattoos as a memorization tool for our ladies in the studio. He liked the idea. And yet, similarly to my best friend blind date, I think the tattoo company owner went into the meeting with different intentions. I went in hoping for partnership, and he was looking to recruit an influencer for his company . . . someone like me. After our conversation, He turned the spotlight on me and said I might be able to help him draw some people into his brand. He wanted to pay me to be *me*.

I didn't know what it entailed to be an "influencer," but before I knew it, we were saying our goodbyes and I told him I would pray into the idea. My conversation later with the Lord was short-lived. The Lord basically pointed me back to my journal where I had asked Him to value me in the world of business. As I continued reading my former entries, I was surprised as He reminded me about my further request: *to be paid for being myself.*

I gladly accepted the position and immediately started sharing the tattoos with new friends anywhere the Lord led me. I spent my days sending e-blasts and making e-friends through online social platforms. E-friends aren't as fun as meeting face-to-face, so I aimed to set up as many in-person meetings as possible. Because the tattoo company had a great following, I got to network with larger companies in town and around the nation. It was fun to see what a lot of businesses were doing on a large scale in my own backyard.

Through my influencer outreach, the Lord started to peel back layers of pain from former jobs and devised a surprise healing plan. No longer was I the one knocking on doors, but people were coming to me! And the cherry on top was my boss friend was *okay* with me promoting my fitness business through connections on his platform. He figured, if he could help both of our businesses grow at the same time, it was a "win" for us all.

The Lord works in peculiar ways. I never knew the day my new boss friend took me out for a cup of chai would be what I needed to launch me into my healing journey. Not only was I getting paid to just "be me," but I was also encouraged to promote my company along the way. I am truly in awe of the Lord's ways, and I am so glad they are not like my own.

Part two of my healing was a bit more of a process. Sometime into my influencer role, the T-shirt company popped up on our social media platform, and a lightbulb went off in my head. If I couldn't partner with them for my studio, maybe they would be interested in temporary tattoos for their business! After all, my friend's company had tens of thousands of followers. Who wouldn't want to partner with us?

After many attempts years prior, I decided to reach out to the T-shirt company one more time, this time as the "face" of the Christian tattoo company. To my surprise, they still took a while to get back to me. Sigh. That did make me feel a bit better as a representative of a much larger brand. They did get back to me eventually, and they apologized for the delay as they navigated new waters as a start-up company. Through some back-and-forth communications, I discovered they were excited to collaborate, and I was in need of some forgiveness in my own heart before delving into our new partnership. I did what I could to forgive and asked the Lord to take care of the rest. After all, there was so much more behind the sickness in my hope-deferred heart. This poor company just so happened to be the silver lining the Lord used to keep chipping away at my embittered heart.

As the partnership progressed, the T-shirt company decided to create their own custom temporary tattoos to show love and support for the families in the wildfires in California. As we created and co-marketed, I got to know their media gal well. We laughed and hit it off. She mentioned their need for models every so often for their product in exchange for free gear. I told her I'd be happy to help.

One ordinary Wednesday shortly after that conversation, I received a surprise text from the media gal asking if I was free Friday or Saturday for a photo shoot. That's how the modeling world goes—lots of last-minute gigs that involve clothing changes in the car out in the middle of an open field or mountain trail. It's not as glamorous as people may think.

I wanted to help, and I had high hopes this was my break to get my foot in the door. I cleared my schedule, and we agreed to meet on Saturday. We set our meeting location for the mall to pick up some last-minute items for the shoot. The store manager was a cute blonde and mentioned she'd be modeling with me. She and some others piled into the large SUV as we headed for the reservoir.

Our team laughed a lot, smiled a lot, and made it through each of our outfit changes. Success! During the car ride back, we were sharing stories, and I was leaning in to grasp all I could from the founder and her business success story. Between the founder and media gal in the front, two male models and me in the middle, and the store manager crammed between all of our outfit changes in the last row of the SUV, we were in tight quarters. Tight spaces tend to cause natural bonding. In our storytelling, somehow I got to sharing about my wild adventures in Africa. I told the story of how my whole business was birthed out of a trip to Mozambique and visiting a gym with a mission to help street boys.

The male model (also an employee at the store) perked up and said he had visited Mozambique around the same time. I don't know how to explain it any other way than the Holy Spirit jogged my memory to recognize the model's face *in that very moment.* It hit me all at once. *I was in Mozambique at the exact same time as this guy.* He and his brother were at one of the workouts one day at the *exact* gym I had visited. We had a full conversation, and they even toured me around their place in Maputo. We both laughed in shock as we recalled meeting two years prior and pondered the chances of a spontaneous reunion at a random photo shoot in Colorado. Jesus likes to sprinkle fun stories into our lives to remind us He is in control, He knows what He's doing, and we can entrust every little detail to Him.

When we returned to the mall, we all hopped in our vehicles as the day replayed in my mind. "Okay, Lord. I get it. You're in control, and I can let go of trying to make things happen." Partnership with the T-shirt company didn't pan out for my fitness studio because the founders moved their headquarters to California a couple months after our shoot. I did get some pretty photos back from the media gal, though. She was quite talented.

About six months went by before I got a text from one of my mentors. She said she and her daughter were shopping at the mall and were wondering if I had done some modeling because they saw a massive ad outside the T-shirt company's storefront with a woman who looked a lot like me. Right then, I received a photo of a blonde hanging from the mall storefront and staring back at me. Sure enough. It was me, larger than life and repping their hat and tee.

What I haven't told you is I always dreamt of modeling for the Lord. I wanted to represent Him and to use the income I made for His Kingdom. Fitness classes in their store at the mall may have never happened, but I nearly fell off my chair when I saw the fifteen-foot-long ad *that did*. And that's a story for another time, but once when I was asking the Lord for a sign that I was in the right place, a bus pulled up right next to me and just so happened to have my face on it from a different photo shoot. Tell me God doesn't have a sense of humor!

I love how Daddy God takes our hurt and pain and turns them into something we could never dream up ourselves. I never thought I would find my face on a mall ad representing the Lord, and one twenty times my natural size, too. So, part two of my healing journey was a massive banner outside a Christian store in a mall. Because I felt seen by the Lord, it was so much better than any fitness class I could have hosted there. As I stared at the banner of myself staring back at me with a big old smile, I surrendered the dream of ever hosting a class in the mall, laughed and told the Lord He had really outdone Himself this time. I didn't know the Bible verse about God doing "immeasurably more than all we ask or imagine" would be literal in size. When Jesus says He wants to do big things, He does. And it's not just big. It's massive!

CHAPTER 27

DELAYS OR DESTINY?

*I*n waiting for Moses to come down from the mountain, the Israelites made a golden calf from their jewelry to form an idol. It was because of impatience. It says verbatim, "When the people saw that Moses was *so long in coming down* from the mountain," is when they decided to take matters into their own hands Exodus 32:1, emphasis mine).

Delays are hard. I had a thirteen-year delay of wanting to move to the ocean. I cannot fathom a forty-year delay like the Israelites experienced. It's easy to take delays personally and to feel like we are doing something wrong. Sometimes we could be. And other times God is still at work on our behalf.

When the Lord finally opened doors for me to move to the beach after thirteen years of waiting, I was ecstatic. Per the usual, Jesus outdid Himself. Not only was I moving to a beach, but I was moving to the best of all beaches—land *surrounded* by beaches on every side on the Big Island of Hawaii. I felt like a celebrity welcomed to the 'aina as the Lord rolled out the red carpet before me. He gave me an affordable bungalow in the jungle with a gazebo overlooking the ocean. He provided every decorative item my heart desired (as they were all pinned on Pinterest). Every. Single. Item. He even provided a sheer white canopy with a bamboo frame over my bed for only $10. My landlord had it tucked away in a closet somewhere, and in our thrifting adventures together, I relayed how it had been a dream of mine since I was five. The Lord connected the dots, and their pile in the corner became my serenity space. And the blessings continued. I was less than ten minutes from a white sand beach with beachside parking. I had community from my former church and several new friends. It was divine.

Yet, before the beauty came the hardships. Prior to stepping foot into my new beach bungalow, I was hit with yet another delay. After the doors closed to Africa twice, unsuccessful relationships and single at thirty-two, a failed business and several job disappointments, I was tired. I was exhausted from putting my hope in what would someday show up. My sick heart from the hope deferred over the prior thirteen years was continually getting sicker. And, it was slightly annoying because, somehow, I still had a faint sense of hope that wouldn't fizzle out. I wanted so badly to let my many dreams and desires go and "cruise," as they say in Hawaii. I wanted to stop dreaming and to see how that might work for a short time. But I couldn't. It's not how the Lord wired me. It's not how He wired any of us because He is the hope in us. He is with us *and* in us. And that little, annoying sense of hope that I felt deep down wasn't a feeling. For the first time, I realized what it meant to have Jesus as my Hope.

My flight to Hawaii was set to leave March 31, 2020. Just before then, the whole world shut down. The COVID-19 pandemic hit, and I was in isolation with my two parents and dog. I didn't see any friends for two months straight. The Lord told me one thing during that time: "Honor your parents." Everything in me wanted to rebel. I wanted to lash out with the pain I had experienced over and over for the past thirteen years. I was *sick of the delay*. The day I found out my flight to Kona was cancelled for the fourth time, I went to hit some tennis balls with my dad. I was so angry I couldn't help but repeatedly hit death balls with every return. (They have a court in their yard, so I was thankful for that outlet.) I think he got a little scared because he calmly suggested that we go inside and play another day. I continued to plow the balls into the fence thinking, *Jesus, I don't understand! Why now? Why couldn't I have left before all of this? What are You doing?*

The next day, I asked forgiveness from the Lord and cried a lot as I listened to a sermon. I realized the Lord had strategy and purpose for me while I was staying with my parents during those two months, and if I couldn't stop it, I would embrace it. That day, I made a list of all the things I had wanted to do in life but never had the time to do because of distractions and busyness. I no longer had an excuse. I couldn't hang out with friends or go anywhere except to workout on the property. It seemed like the most beautiful opportunity to chase down some goals.

During those two months, I ended up reading five books, started writing this one, learned guitar, made some macramé creations, watched movies with family, and played tennis with Dad after taking hour-long walks with Mom followed by the "Megan and Judy" cooking show. We didn't really have a show, but we might as well have. We got so crafty in the kitchen that we started to share recipes with our extended family members. We could have had our own cookbook with all we whipped up.

The fact that I can even write those statements are a miracle in and of themselves. If you asked my closest friends, they would tell you I had very little hope in my heart that my relationship with my parents would ever change. We were just *different*.

They were introverts. I was an extrovert. They were thinkers. I was a dreamer. They worked nine-to-five jobs. I was an entrepreneur. We didn't seem to have a lot in common, and as Jesus so painfully revealed to me, I was the one who was getting in the way of our relationship. It was *my heart* that needed healing. I wanted it. I just didn't know how.

The beauty and challenge about inviting the Lord into our process is it can't be fully reproduced, meaning He works one way for me and another for you. Healing is not a "one-size-fits-all" kind of a process like we sometimes teach in church, business or the world. We can't put Him in a box. Yet, one step I *know* works for *everyone* is repentance and surrender. When we fully give over an area of our hearts to the Lord and ask Him to change it, He will. We might fight the process, but when we say *yes* to Him, He will allow pain to come temporarily so the ugly can leave. And it leaves us healed, whole, and fully alive. The pain is worth the journey. It's worth the joy on the other side. It's more than worth the thirteen-year wait for the seven-minute drive to the beach and jungle bungalow in the mountains of Hawaii.

Even better than the blessings of ocean waves and sun-kissed skin was the lasting change in my heart toward both of my parents. Prior to the move, I had never been homesick in my life. I started sleepovers with friends at age three, and every time my parents left growing up, it was no problem. I have always been independent. Yet, when I got to Hawaii in my little bungalow filled with everything I had ever longed for, I started to really miss Mom and Dad. I missed the long walks with Mom while she shared stories about her dad on the farm. I missed poking fun at Dad when he whiffed a tennis ball. (Because he truly is a rock star tennis player with great technique, and someone had to give him a hard time.) I missed daydreaming with Mom about what was for dinner and what new creation we would come up with next. I missed lounging on the couch and scrolling Netflix as we contemplated the next movie to watch since we had seen nearly all of them.

I never would have felt all these things had my heart not been transformed during those two pandemic months. I don't know how it happened. It just did. I said, "Transform my heart." Jesus said, "Okay." He took the selfishness out of me and gave me eyes to see my parents from His perspective. And for the first time, I saw them as *my friends*.

When we are frustrated, Jesus is always the answer. I don't know how He does it, but what I can explain is this: It's worth it. Any hurt and pain from hope deferred is worth it because He's doing a work in us that only He can do. The healing will far surpass the blessings on the other side. It will bring more joy, more peace, and more freedom than any *thing* or *experience* He could ever give. And as you know, we have a wonderful and giving Father.

I love how He's a "both and" kind of God. He *both* gives us the fruit in our hearts *and* gives us the tangible blessings on the other side of the healing. Daddy God reminds me of a parent at the dinner table with his children who just ate their green beans, and He's congratulating us with a big, gooey cookie for the job well done in bringing health to our bodies. Health and freedom are a choice. It's not the easy road, but maybe that's why the Lord likes to congratulate us along the way.

There is no question that He is for us. He is for you. If you're still awaiting fruit of any kind, know and believe *it is coming*. Don't fight the process. The journey is where He is, and it's where we get to create memories with others, too. Whatever your "pandemic season" represents, He's in it. That's not the question. The question is, *will you surrender?* Will you ask for eyes to see heaven's perspective and for the grace to love the people He's placed around you? He's got you there for a purpose and on purpose. It *will* transform you, one delay at a time. Maybe we should stop calling them delays and start calling them blessings.

CHAPTER 28

SPIRITUAL DEFIBRILLATOR

*I*t turns out that slowing down—and I mean way down—makes you confront "your stuff." I knew moving to Hawaii meant healing, but I didn't realize it meant coming face-to-face with all the hope deferred and trauma I had endured throughout the previous ten years of my life.

You know the feeling when you see red and blue lights in your rearview mirror and your heart sinks? Or when you pass a police car on the road and immediately hit the brakes? Law enforcement more than intimidated me growing up. I had a fear of authority, almost to an unhealthy point. The moment I knew my heart was in deep and painful waters was when I was pulled over in my first week adventuring in my new state. The Big Island of Hawaii has one main highway that connects the north and south. It's really the only way to get anywhere. I was going fifteen miles per hour over the speed limit due to my "mainland" tendencies that trained me to go sixty-five (or maybe seventy) in the fast lane. On the Big Island, no road exceeds fifty-five, which the police officer wasn't shy to inform me as he approached my window. Believe it or not, I kept *trying* to ease my foot off the pedal, but it was as if my foot were a weight stuck in a certain position while driving. Try telling that to a cop in your new hometown. I'm sure he's heard that one a time or two.

Getting pulled over wasn't the scary part. Getting a ticket in the first week out of quarantine also wasn't the worst part. Subconsciously, I heard a small voice whisper, *Slow down. You're going to get pulled over*, about five minutes prior to it happening. Not kidding. The more time we spend with the Lord, the more we hear His soft, sweet whispers—and warnings. The problem was I was so numb from all the pain of ten years of loss and unfulfilled dreams that *I just didn't care anymore*—about anything, even my once-paralyzing fear of authority. I was numb, and neither good nor bad seemed to phase me.

I hopped on the phone with a friend after getting a semi-reduced ticket with a rather unmerciful cop. I told her I was in trouble. My heart couldn't feel. I am hardwired to feelings and vulnerability. It's how God created me, and I've learned to steward it well over the years. Up until that point, I hadn't been pulled over a lot, but enough to know the slight panicked feeling that came along with being in the wrong. This time, I felt nothing—absolutely *nothing*.

After thanking the officer and hanging up with my friend, I continued toward my original destination, the beach. The warm waves and sun were medicine to my aching soul those first three months, and then something happened. That same numbness with the police officer trickled into other areas of my life: my restaurant job, my worship nights I held at my house, even my ability to wake up with a sense of purpose. I usually tend toward optimism, but I had to be honest with my heart. I was depressed. The book of Ecclesiastes never felt so real: Life truly felt *meaningless*. Reading that part of scripture never felt truer, and quite honestly, it seemed to feed the depression.

My feelings, or lack thereof, made absolutely no sense. Jesus had brought to life some of my thirteen-year-long-awaited dreams of living in a beachy bungalow. He "rolled out the red carpet" for me, in the words of one of my friends. I had the opportunity to lavishly decorate with the Lord and received exactly everything I desired. He made things happen that I didn't think were physically possible, like getting to do daily life with my incredible neighbors who offered me the ohana next to them. I even got the long-awaited RAV4 I'd been praying for on the mainland for over two years.

I had one of the most supportive friend groups I had ever experienced surrounding me, loving me well, and even looking to me with honor and inspiration. And yet, I was awaiting changes and successes in my business abilities, continuously hoping to meet my husband I had dreamt of since age three and surrendered countless times over ten years, and believing for visionary doors to open for just *the* next step. Therein was the problem. It wasn't until I was lavishly provided for in my ocean "Promised Land," with every concrete interior design dream of my heart, that I came face-to-face with some realities. Yes, the Lord was faithful. Yes, He cared for me way more than the birds of the air and flowers of the field. He proved Himself faithful over and over, and I trusted in Him. I was thankful for the solid friendship and foundation I had built with Him, *yet I had a hope and purpose issue.*

Hope deferred made my heart sick. It was true. Depression is a sickness and a tricky one at that, because the symptoms are mostly internal. In today's world, it can be easy for some of us to put on a smile and cover up our sick hearts. I did. It wasn't until the Lord took me into the "slow lane" with some red and blue lights that I realized I needed a spiritual defibrillator. The thing about defibrillators is that you can't shock yourself. You need someone to assist you. Jesus was kind enough to show me I needed assistance, and He was first in line to help.

Mental health is a sticky topic. I think there is a time and a place for medication. All I know is my own journey, and I decided to follow the path out to Hawaii that the Lord laid in front of me. I have another dear friend who lost her business and found herself in a similar "funk." Jesus dealt her a different card and blessed her with a full year-and-a-half's salary on medical leave while He rolled out the red carpet for her to attend a quality treatment program. Now, she's thriving, living by the ocean and a master saleswoman with a passion to help others in their mental health journey. It's different for all of us, but the Lord knows what He's doing. I've learned not to keep questioning His process. Just read the book of Job to understand why.

Part of healing is confronting some of our "ugly" so that Jesus can wash it away and we can become clean and *free*. It's like the old silver china set my mom used to have. We polished it as a chore every year before Thanksgiving or Christmas. My mom was smart and taught us the value of a dollar and budgeting back then, so she would pay us for each chore we chose. I didn't think rubbing a silver china set was worth the $0.75 of the effort put in, so I settled for the bigger jobs like washing the kitchen floor for $1.25. Either way, it was always cool to see the transformation of the china set when my sister was done polishing. It went from streaks of black in the hidden corners to shiny and squeaky clean. It reminds me of that scene from *Beauty and the Beast* when the dishes and chandelier are dancing in all their glory. There's something about seeing dirty things become beautiful that's appealing. We are hardwired for transformation —to become more like Jesus.

The hard part of transformation is coming to terms with *knowing* a shift needs to occur. That's where the buffing comes in, and it's usually not easy and might not appear beautiful, either. In fact, usually it's the point where the darkest and grimiest areas are exposed all at once. My grime was like one of the churches in Revelation where Jesus says His "beef" with them was they had forsaken their first love (see Revelation 2:4). They had put other things in front of Him. They had chosen goals and to-do lists and even *people* or *things* over Him. The Lord revealed in a sweet and gentle way while bringing me to my dream ocean bungalow that my heart was sick because I had put my hope in the wrong place. My purpose was in the dreams of my heart. In circumstances. In outcomes. In people. In *things*. I had seen dream after dream after dream die, and by the time a long-awaited dream came to pass, my heart was already so hurt that it felt on the verge of death itself.

I once heard a podcast talking about marriages that were fizzling out and how the women had become so hurt over time that their hearts turned bitter. I've experienced bitterness before, and I never want to go back. After years and years of the couples idling in bitterness without attempting to heal their marriages, they decided to attend therapy. The therapist gathered the men from the study group and came up with an idea where each man could do something nice for his wife each week (after years of not doing these kind acts). The result of the study was interesting. The women lashed out and were not able to receive the kind acts from their husbands because there was too much damage already done and their hearts were too hard and embittered to receive the generosity.

I think I found myself in that camp, so hurt that my heart decided to just shut off. In fact, I was in it while typing portions of this book. The only thing I have known to try is writing and inviting the Lord into it all. I tell everyone I know to journal. It's one of the most healing ways to experience Jesus because He meets us right where we are. If not writing, it's whatever brings your heart to life with Him.

I don't know that we, as a church, have done the best job at having genuine conversations about depression and heartache. We can tend to get uncomfortable with the topic and almost "prosperity gospel" our way to a false sense of hope, putting on a smile while our hearts are feeling a whole different story. I have found I cannot always trust my feelings, but at the same time, we were created in God's image, and our feelings are a good thermometer for how our hearts are doing.

There's a time to press into the pain, and there's a time to pick ourselves off the floor and proclaim truth and pray Scripture over our minds. There's a time to sit back in the lap of Jesus and let Him do the comforting, and there's a time to armor up and storm the gates of hell by drawing on our history with the Lord knowing that He is faithful. *Because He is.* It's why creating memories with the Lord is so important. It's why spending those first waking moments with Him and conversing with Him throughout the day are life and death to our souls. It's a life-long, two-way relationship with a Friend who listens to your every word. And you will *know* it because He *will* respond if you truly desire to do life with Him. Unlike us carnal beings, He really does have the capacity for every word we speak. Every. Single. Word. Every request. Every tear. Every dream. Every longing. He cares. He's just waiting for *us* to make a move toward Him. He's already made every move thinkable toward us.

Creating history and trust with the Lord in the small things tethers our roots to endure the big ones. The cancer. The job layoff. The depression. The lists go on and on. Jesus didn't promise that we wouldn't have trouble or pain. He did the opposite and said, "In this world you *will* have trouble (John 16:33)." But He didn't leave us there. He continued, "But take heart! I have overcome the world." There's joy in knowing our Best Friend overcomes the trouble *with* us.

Sometimes God points me to Scripture by speaking to me through numbers. Everywhere I've turned in this past healing season, I see "10:10." The numbers are blaringly repetitive on a clock, in my readings, and even during the job hunt for serving jobs listed with a base of $10.10. It immediately reminded me of a mentor's favorite Bible verse from a former season and the promise that awaits us. In John 10:10, Jesus talked about the thief coming "to steal and kill and destroy." That definitely resonated with the majority of the last ten years of my life. But, again, He didn't stop there. The latter part of the verse is the promise where He said, "I have come that they may have life, and have it to the full." I think it's His reminder for me not to give up and to trust Him when my emotions (or lack thereof) seem to be shouting the loudest. When we *feel* like we are on shifting sand, the Lord wants us to know what is true. I'm learning that scriptures aren't just words. By walking these roads with the Lord, we get to claim the words as an unshakeable foundation for our own journey.

This season of depression was new. It was uncomfortable. It made me draw on everything I have ever known. At the end of the day, I know that I know that *I know* God is faithful. I know that He's kind, despite the lies the enemy tries to tell me. I know that He cries with me when I'm sad, and I have even felt Him nudging me to "dream again," even though I don't know how. I don't know what inspires me anymore. It's a good thing He does. He knows me better than I know myself. He knows why He created me. He knows that I have a purpose, and He keeps telling me to "dream bigger."

That's what He told me when I proclaimed from the pulpit I would be the founder of the largest Christian fitness studio in the world. I had to shut down my business five months later. Talk about a blow to the heart and ego. Yet, amid the business shut down, my Biggest Fan and Business Coach told me to "dream bigger."

If I had not *known* the character of my Champion and Friend who pushes me to achieve my wildest dreams with a tangible triathlon suit, I would not have believed that He was for me in this season of depression. But I can't deny the facts. He *is* my Biggest Proponent and Wildest Dreamer of my dreams. He outdreams me every time. And *I know* He wants my heart to heal *more than I do*. But it takes effort on my part. It takes surrendering control and letting go of unknown outcomes where I've already premeditated my own ending. It takes handing it over to Him to let Him write the "happily ever after" for me. It takes seeking relationship with Him day in and day out, before pursuing anything else.

I stand on the truths from the Bible. I also stand on my personal encounters and experiences with Jesus because those are real to me. I have to be genuine with my heart, and my heart knows the mountains and the valleys where the Lord has walked with me. I love the mountaintop experiences. I loved the day I got to pop champagne in the studio the Lord provided for *free* in the exact location I prayed for when opening my first studio location. I also have loved the moments I sobbed my eyes out after a breakup and felt the warm Presence of the Lord deeper than any other tangible experience in this life. I don't love this apathetic state my heart has found, especially in the most beautiful blue ocean waters in the United States, but I know I won't be here forever. I know that in turning to the Lord and asking Him to deliver me, He will, because that's what He does. He creates beauty from ashes and gives us joy in the mourning.

Even if I can't understand His ways (and I never fully will), I still choose to trust. I still choose to pursue. I still choose to believe. I cannot fully grasp the concept that He is strong in my weakness, but I know His character, and He always shows up. He's always listening, and He's always there, even when I cannot feel Him. I know that through every valley and every loss, He has *always* brought me through, buffed me up, and made me more beautiful on the other side. He does it every time I give him my *yes*. God is in the beauty and health business, just not in the way the world sees beauty.

The moments I decide to press into Him are the times I get to see myself transform before my very eyes into the beautiful butterfly on the other side. I've seen myself respond differently in situations where I would have otherwise been offended or fallen victim to my circumstances. I'm learning that the "rebirth" of a Christian is more of a process and less of a "say some words to believe" kind of a thing. Yes, I believe there is a moment in time where we accept Jesus as Savior and ask Him to forgive and change us from our old ways, but I truly am learning how much we must continue to choose Him moment by moment to transform. We can't remain babies forever. Babies grow to become full adults, and with our growth come choices.

Love is a choice. Relationship is a choice. Transformation is a choice. As we invite Jesus into a new area of our hearts, He will press in and do the transforming so we become more and more like Him in that area of our hearts. But we must choose. And there are so many areas that we get to invite Him into. With that choosing also comes the "ugly." It's inevitable because we must unlearn the not-so-pretty things we've picked up along the way.

But in the healing and stormy seasons of life, there is always, *always* a rainbow on the other side.

We live for the rainbows. It's why we sit through an hour and a half of pain and gore in a movie to see the five-minute victory at the end. We are wired for victory. And we know who the Ultimate Victor of this world is. What's wild is *we get an invitation* into that victory. I believe heaven on earth can happen here and now. I live to see people set free. It's why Jesus died. Not so that we can live in shackles of pain. He died so we can live free *now*. It's awaiting us. You have an invitation to freedom. I have an invitation to freedom. I choose *yes* to relationship with Him above all else. No matter how "wired" I am to "do," He keeps telling me to "be." And in my "being," He does the "doing" that leads to my transforming.

Yes, depression is real. Yes, cancer is real. Yes, trauma and abuse are real. And so is Jesus. He cares. He's close, even if we don't feel Him.

There were moments where my rebellious and religious heart strived to get into His Presence to no avail. And then there were the moments where I cried out in desperation. I learned guitar during the pandemic, and after wandering in circles and not connecting with the Lord through the Word or out on a run, I picked up the guitar and poured out my heart to Him long into the night. My song was simple, "My soul longs to be near You. But Your arms feel so far. My heart needs reviving. To laugh, to love, to cry. And You're the only One who can try." I sang it over and over. I bet David was looking down from heaven saying, "Yep, I feel you, sister. Just pour out your heart. He's got you."

And then there were the mornings where I woke up and things just seemed easier and different. My desert season lasted years and even transferred to Hawaii. A friend called it my "desert in paradise." It was difficult to feel the Lord in any capacity during my depression. One morning after battling two different viruses along with suffering battle wounds from a surfing crash, I felt an invitation to sit with Jesus instead of hitting the beach. *I chose Him.* I wasn't connecting with Him through Scripture, so I turned on worship. It's important to know the artists the Lord speaks through to break into your heart. Mine has always been Steffany Gretzinger, because she soothed my heart and soul as I surrendered my dream of the studio (the first time) at the conference in Colorado Springs so many years ago. I scrolled and found a song I had never heard, "This Close," as her words depicted my every thought and current experience in that moment.

The song mentions how God doesn't struggle to hear us, so we don't have to strive to be heard. I *knew* the Lord was catching my every word because He knows every thought and dream I have uttered, and even those I haven't. I knew because He came through, and I was sitting in the long-awaited ocean bungalow promise after thirteen years of waiting.

Something shifted in my heart as, for the first time in a long while, Gretzinger's words *felt* true in the depths of my soul while I was not able to feel anything at all. She finishes with a profound line that when we *feel* like our faith is "going under," for the Lord to intervene and remind us we are known.

And you know what? He did. He brought to mind an image of a sapphire ring He had given me. Though I didn't feel His strong Presence, I got to sit there knowing that He saw me. He *saw me.* He knew my faith felt like it was going under, and He was faithful to remind me I am known. I am desired. I am His Bride. And so are you.

Invite Him into the pain and be real with your emotions and heart. Yet don't let yourself dwell too long in the pit to give the enemy a stronghold over you. Ask the Lord to remind you

you're known. Put on whatever song or movie or read whatever book or hike whatever path you've explored with the Lord in creating your own history with Him.

I saw victory over depression. It wasn't overnight, but there's purpose in His timeline and His way. The Lord wanted to sit with me in my "House up on a Hill" (another good song in my tough season by Amanda Lindsey Cook). He wanted me to draw, not on my feelings, but on my history I've created with Him. It's part of renewing my mind, and I believe it's part of my "rebirth" as pieces of me die one by one and fall away to make me new again, but this time *in Him*.

Feelings aren't bad. They are an indicator of what's really going on in our hearts, but they cannot determine the course of our hearts. Our history with the Lord can. That's what the Bible is. It's history of so many others who have gone before us and how the Lord has faithfully shown up for them. Look at David. He led a life of crazy victory as he slayed his "ten thousands" (1 Samuel 18:8). And yet, he also sat with an aching heart time and time again, crying out to the Lord in his longings. Just read the Psalms. I think we forget about those parts of the Bible in light of our own journeys. The Lord made it clear in writing this book to share the highs *and* the lows, depression, and all. It's been two and a half years since I lost my business. In the grand scheme of things, that is a drop in the bucket, but to my heart, it feels like eternity.

I know one thing to be true: My heart *will* dream again. And in the sweet moments in the house up on the hill when He whispered, "You are known," I chose to listen and respond, even if I didn't feel like it, because I know who holds my heart. I trust Him with everything inside me because He's proven Himself over and over and over. He doesn't have to. He chooses to. That's Someone I want to put my hope in now and always.

My childhood dream of a canopy bed finally
unfolding nearly 25 years later in my beachy
bungalow bedroom.

TRAIT XII

KEEPER OF MY HEART

CHAPTER 29

WEDDING SURPRISES

*P*eople would ask why I moved to Hawaii, and depending on who was asking, I would tell them, "To honeymoon with Jesus." I knew I was entering into an engagement and marriage season with the Lord. I had no idea what it entailed, but what better place to honeymoon than Hawaii?

The first three months we explored the beaches by day and wrote this book by night. I didn't try to make any friends. I just wanted to be with Him. The Lord was so gracious, and He brought me friends anyway!

My friend groups seemed to transition a lot on the island. I've learned that people come and go, but I was caught off guard with the sudden change in direction for my sweet neighbors after three short months together. They felt the Lord tugging at their hearts to transition from their Hawaii home to Texas. I joined the packing and cleaning party because I wanted every excuse to be with them before the big move. As my friend loaded up their large suitcases, she started a "discard pile" that continued to grow as she tossed aside shorts, swimsuits, and bohemian-looking pants you might find in a market in Thailand. She would say, "Try that one on! This one would look great on you," as she continued to separate the items. Then, she came around the corner and said, "I've been wanting to give this to you." It was my favorite long, sheer white dress of hers I had tried on the year prior when I visited for a few short weeks, but my practical Colorado-self couldn't bring myself to buy it at the time. She handed it to me and said, "It's yours."

In any other season of life, even a year ago, it would have been simply a lacy white dress. In this clearly defined season, it was now my wedding dress. I couldn't believe it! Jesus had gifted me a wedding dress through my generous neighbor and friend. I thought to myself, *So this is what it means to "be Jesus" to others*, as I thanked the Lord for her generosity and His kindness.

Later that day, I left for my bi-monthly Costco trip to fill up on gas and pick up some extra coconut milk and veggies. Upon entering, I struck up a conversation with a nice guy who I thought was a Costco worker, seeing as he was twinning with them in his bright orange vest. I discovered he had just gotten off of work in construction. We parted ways, and I continued along my rat race as I turned corner after corner, making my way through the maze and picking up items along the way. As I hurried to the conveyor belt finish line to get my place in line, someone tapped me on the shoulder. I turned around thinking, *Who on earth would know me at Costco in Hawaii*, seeing as I had only lived there for a few short months. It was my new friend, Cyrus, wearing his bright orange vest and a big smile on his face as he handed me a large bouquet of beautiful flowers. I thanked him, in awe of his random act of kindness. I can honestly say this was my first experience receiving flowers from a complete stranger. I was stunned!

On my drive home, I was smiling from ear-to-ear, knowing exactly who the flowers were from. I had enough experience in receiving flowers from the Lord to know they weren't *just* from my new friend Cyrus. They were from Jesus! What are the chances I would receive a white dress *and* a bouquet of flowers on the exact same day? It amazes me how the Lord can partner with anything and anyone to pursue our hearts.

When I returned home, I shared the story with my sweet neighbor. As a photographer, she decided it might be fun to document my wedding season with the Lord before she moved off island. The white dress made the photos, but due to our busy schedules, the flowers did not. Some things we can only take with us in memory.

After our island photo shoot, I was reminded in my journaling how an old Colorado roommate, just as wild in her faith, was in a similar "engagement" season with the Lord just before meeting her husband. She told me a story of how she really wanted a ring from the Lord in her engagement season as she was learning to be His Bride. She prayed boldly, and two weeks later, she got a ring in the mail! The envelope had no return address, no nothing, except her name and a ring in it. And guess what? The ring only fit her ring finger.

With that story in mind, I felt prompted to boldly ask the Lord for a ring, too, if He'd be so kind. I felt spoiled already, yet I prayed in faith for an engagement ring, knowing it would complete my wedding season. I wrote out my request to the Lord, not even sure what kind of ring I wanted.

Two weeks later, my season of humility continued as I scrubbed toilets and showers and mopped floors for a woman who offered me a job. She told me when and where to show up and didn't give me a choice to refuse the job. I guess that's how you know you're supposed to be in something; Jesus just doesn't give you a choice! I stepped into the opportunity, grateful to have a job as a new island resident. I came to love it there. Her home became like a second home to me and secretly fulfilled my "Blue Crush" dreams I had desired since seeing the movie in high school. I was living the island life.

There were weeks I really didn't feel like scrubbing another toilet, don't get me wrong, but for the most part, the Lord met me in really powerful ways through songs or podcasts each week. Several weeks went by before I went to do a full "under the bed" clean. We had to work our way through an inch of dust atop her cabinets and ceiling fans before I could get to the dust bunnies under the bed.

When I finally got down on my knees to assess "the situation," I found something round that could have been a small animal or spider, but I didn't want to suck it up in case it was something of value. I took a broom and swept it out from under the bed.

Through the dust, I could still make out a shiny blue oval ring surrounded by white diamonds. I just laughed as I thought back to my prayer. I stuck it on my finger thinking, "Well, I didn't specify if I would be the owner of the ring. I just asked for a ring, and if I only get to wear it for a few hours while I clean, that's good enough for me."

At the end of my cleaning shift, my *hanai* (Hawaiian for adopted) mom thanked me for cleaning, and I handed her the ring. She said, "Oh, do you know what this ring is? It's the ring I bought that's the exact replica of Princess Diana's engagement ring!" I looked at the sapphire stone remembering back to the days of Princess Diana, and before I knew it, she handed the ring to me and said, "Keep it. It's yours."

I was shocked and said while laughing, "You have no idea what you just did," as I told her the story of the white dress and flowers. She just smiled as if she was already in on some engagement surprise only she and Jesus knew about. I was baffled and chuckling all at the same time as I remembered the "ask and you shall receive" verses from the Bible (Matthew 7:7; Luke 11:9).

Being on the receiving end of a blessing is fun. I get ecstatic! But I'm learning that even more fun than receiving is giving. As I read back through these chapters of the Lord's faithfulness, and in my current season of serving others, I'm realizing how "me-centered" these stories are. And there's no shame in it because the Lord loves us and wants to romance our hearts. That's *how* I created my deep foundation of trust with Him. It's my favorite trait about Him—how He pursues my heart. But it doesn't stop there. I'm learning how relationship goes so much deeper when we are invested and get to serve the other person, joyfully. *I get to love Him back.* And for the first time, I understand I *get* to be part of the story so others can experience what I've experienced all these years. We all have access to His blessings, and He knows us better than we know ourselves. As the givers, we just get to listen and joyfully obey when the Lord says "give."

With Christmas approaching, I felt the Lord prompt my heart three different times through social media posts or just "random" passing thoughts to reach out to a distant friend and offer her my beachy bungalow for her honeymoon while I was visiting home for the holidays. I figured one month prior to their wedding they surely already had their honeymoon plans purchased and set in stone. Heck, they probably already had their bags packed and ready. But I decided to be obedient and "look a fool," knowing the several times I'd felt so *seen* by the Lord in such intimate ways were because of someone else's obedience (whether they knew it or not).

We never know what someone else is walking through. Jesus does. So, when He prompts us to reach out, it's probably because the person on the receiving end is about to get insanely blessed. Who wants to skip out on that opportunity? Not me!

This friend got back to me right away. I could feel her excitement through the phone as she relayed that her honeymoon plans were cancelled the week prior with all the unknowns of the pandemic and the second lockdown on the horizon. We coordinated plans, and before I knew it, she had two confirmed roundtrip tickets to honeymoon at my bungalow during Christmas week. I can honestly say after years of receiving from the Lord, my heart got *more* excitement out of planning every last detail, from the white pedals dusting the floor upon entry to the fresh leis in the fridge and bottle of her favorite wine, than it did in receiving the white dress, flowers, and ring. Of course, I loved the ring and cherished the gifts from the Lord, and even more, feeling *seen* by Him, but this was different. I was in a new season where the joy of giving outgrew the joy of receiving. I got to experience what the Lord probably experiences every time we happen upon a surprise gift from Him. I imagine His heart flutters as tears fall from our eyes. To give from that place is to experience the heart of God on a whole new level.

I think there also comes a time when we get so filled up by the Lord that we must pour it back out to experience that same "high" we once received. It's how He wired us. Jesus Himself told us, "It is more blessed to give than to receive" (Acts 20:35). I have had the pleasure of experiencing both. You can too because, as it turns out, we are all His favorites.

CHAPTER 30

SO IN LOVE

I didn't think I'd get to see the depression lift while writing this book. I surrendered the outcome. But God is *that* good. It's as if He wants me to share hope with you or something. Weird, huh?

It did. It lifted. Completely and totally. And so did the spiritual oppression I was under. It's hard to explain, but it was like a heavy blanket on my soul. It was very real. *And* God was and is bigger. Every time.

I know that I am in a marriage season and about to meet my husband. I've asked the Lord to make it very clear when that time comes. He has. In so many ways, including my marriage season with Him first. I told the Lord I was scared that, with my apathetic heart, I wouldn't be able to *feel* the courtship of my husband, which was devastating to a hopeless romantic gal who's been dreaming of Prince Charming swooping her off her feet since she saw her first Disney movie. I was afraid my heart would be shut off, the same way it was with the policeman.

When Scripture says, "Ask and you shall receive," the old adage, "Be careful what you ask for," can become very true.

God's timing is perfect, and because I'm a "dates and numbers" kind of a gal, He made it very clear He was answering my bold prayer to turn my heart back on with the start of the new year.

New Year's Day, I was working at the restaurant as a barista in Hawaii. It was a job the Lord called me to, and I saw Him work all kinds of miracles with my *ohana* family in the restaurant. It was the busiest day yet, with all the tourists out and about trying to flee the full COVID shutdowns on the Mainland. We were "slammed" to say the least. As I was bagging an over-flowing trash can, a handsome, tall, tan, and tatted local guy came up and said, "I can take that for you."

I thought nothing of it and laughed, "I got it," knowing the dumpster was half a football field away. After all, it was my job. He pushed back and said, "No, I got it."

That's when something broke. I can't explain the way the Lord works. All I know is He doesn't like to be put in a box, nor do I ever want to be the one who boxes Him up. For the first time in three years of no dating (except one friend-date in Denver) and not being attracted to anyone, my heart was fluttering when the man pushed back and showed that one small act of kindness. Who knew a handsome man taking out the trash would flip on the switch in my heart?

I danced the whole rest of the day. One day turned into two. Then three. Then a week. I found myself dancing everywhere I went. I knew this man wasn't my husband for a few different reasons. Yet God can work through anyone. He uses people to shift our hearts. It doesn't mean we skip to conclusions and marry that person the next day. I fasted, prayed, and came to peace with knowing the Lord was up to good things, but the dude wasn't my forever guy. God was answering my prayer and showing me my heart was now open.

I went to church later that week and hadn't felt so near to the Lord since He first encountered me on my parents' basement carpet many years ago. He was washing me with His love, and overwhelming joy bubbled up. I danced. And the dancing didn't stop. My coworkers must have thought I was on drugs or something. I was living in my own kind of musical. I felt like I was floating, and the joy *had* to be released. I was in love. I felt like Buddy the Elf, "I love you, I love you, I *love* you!!!" It might sound crazy to you, but it's the realest emotion I had ever felt. It's that same feeling I felt for the first time in my travel extravaganzas curled up on the airport seat with Jesus, *only better*.

You know those married couples who hold hands and gaze into each other's eyes after fifty years of marriage and say, "It just keeps getting better"? That's because it does. True love really does keep getting better. Jesus keeps getting better. I cannot wait to continue traversing the world and dancing to country songs in the kitchen with my favorite Better Half twenty years from now. Oh, the places we'll go!

Oh, and here's the fun part. The Lord not only lifted the depression and oppression, He showed me *why* I went through that season. He didn't have to, but I asked, and He chose to answer. He doesn't always do that. Again, I think He wants me to share His perspective with you because He cares and He *really is kind*. He really does love you beyond anything you can imagine.

It's simple, really. He delivered me into my kind of Promised Land, but I couldn't feel Him. It's probably similar to what Solomon experienced, with all the riches in the world and more women than he knew what to do with (minus the relational part for me). Solomon had everything at his fingertips, and yet he saw that this life was meaningless and "but a mist." Yes, I have a purpose. You have a purpose. But I hate to break it to you. God does not *need* us. He *wants* us. He wants to be your

Dance Partner and Defibrillator and Biggest Champion. He wants to be the Shoulder you cry on and the One you pop champagne with when you make that big break.

Nothing is worth it without Him. And it's not fun without Him either. Nothing is. Not even the most perfect beachy bungalow only seven minutes away from some of the best beaches with some of the greatest friends in the world. If we aren't careful, once we receive our long-awaited blessings, they can tend to take His place. I think this depression was allowed as a warning to get my heart right before we did anything else together.

Now I know, I don't want any of it if I don't have Him. And I've told Him that. My "desert in paradise" season was a "wake up call" to continue to do life with Him first. He is first place. Best Friends always are. They never move to second place. It's funny that the Lord continues to use trash and toilet seats to give me the greatest revelations in life. I think there's something to that. After all, He *is* the most servant-hearted Trash & Recycle Man alive. He turns even the dirtiest trash into the most beautiful treasure.

CHAPTER 31

BLOWING BUBBLES

The depth of the Lord's heart is vast and never ending. His character continues to astound me as I experience new and different parts of His being. He is all twelve of the traits I explored and more, and all at the same time. Yet it's taken me a quarter of my life to get to know just these aspects. The history I've created with Him leaves me reeling for more because I *know* there is oodles and oodles more, and it really does keep getting better.

I used to be the little girl glued to the screen when anything Disney was playing. I would romanticize how the longing in a princess's heart was fulfilled when love-at-first-sight actualized as Prince Charming fell from the sky. I now know that Disney isn't reality. Or is it? The Lord recently told me through the new releases of our childhood flicks to "start dreaming for my Prince Charming" again.

I am single and thirty-two as I write this, and I can honestly say my first thought was, *But Lord, I'm going to miss this season of singleness with You.* I know my husband is coming, *and* I know I've already found Him. His name is Jesus, and He is my first Love. He is everything my heart has desired through my hundreds of lists. He is ever emotionally available, ever generous, ever kind, ever encouraging, ever selfless, ever humble, and ever free. No one will ever measure up, and they shouldn't because only Jesus can have that place in our hearts.

I'm on that fifty-year, romantic marriage track with the Lord, and it's *because* I've created a whole library of memories with Him. I get to fall deeper and deeper in love with who He is every single day of my life because love is a choice and I have seen the character and goodness of His heart. I have seen the ways He responds to hard circumstances and good ones. And when life doesn't make sense and things go unexplained, He holds me tight and reminds me *He* is the Lord of the Universe and I can leave those details to Him. Even depression can't steal His compassionate hugs. I don't understand it, but He reminds me it's above my pay grade and all I need to do is "*be*" with Him. He's the doer. I'm the be-er. He orchestrates it all into a beautiful symphony, and I get to sit back, watch, and listen.

Jesus said when He comes back, He is looking for faith in the earth (Luke 18:8). As we have learned together, faith is a substance. That means it can be "caught" and, therefore, is something that can be shared, grown, and spread. I invite you to grab hold of that substance and believe for your dreams, day-to-day miracles, or maybe for a big life change. Whatever it is, start small and hold on tight with the utmost boldness, obedience, and belief. And I mean the kind of belief where you know that you know that you know that something is going to happen before it does. That means acting on that belief. Jesus can give us a triathlon suit, but we still must step forward, train, and listen to our Coach.

Relationship with God is just that, a relationship. If you want to experience friendship with Jesus on the same level that I have in these pages, it's easy! Just ask Him right now. He has shown us the greatest act of love there ever will be, in dying for us while we were still going about life in our own selfish ways. He loves you right where you are. You just get to respond by saying *yes* to Him being your forever adventure buddy. It may seem strange, but if you feel led, ask Him right now by uttering the most exciting words of all time: "Jesus, I believe who You say You are. Come and be Lord of my life. Come adventure with me through it all." Amen!

Take the leap. Pray the bold prayer. Train for the race. Quit the job. Or don't. Do what He's leading you to do. One "leap of faith" will lead to another, and before you know it, ten years will fly by, and you'll be walking out your own bold faith stories. It all starts with one step. Life is about the journey as you create your own library of memories with Him.

And don't forget to have fun, bragging on Him along the way. The Lord tells us through the prophet Jeremiah, if we are to boast about anything, it should be that we understand and know Him (Jeremiah 9:24). The Lord also knows that life is more enjoyable with people and our stories are meant to be shared. That's probably why His Word says that "faith comes by hearing," because we need people around to hear and be heard.

Along this journey, I have learned faith has a compounding effect. As we share our own faith stories with one another, it grows more faith in the room. It's like when you see a group of kids blowing bubbles that often float together to create larger bubbles. Small bubbles combine to form larger bubbles. Like the bubbles, faith produces greater faith, which expands to a size that people cannot help but notice. To "faith it forward" is to step out in faith with God and then share your stories with others, spurring on more faith in the room. Your stories are a unique expression of who you are, and no story is too small for a large and passionate God. Remember the mustard seed of faith in the Bible? It moved mountains (Matthew 17:20).

Jesus will capture your attention in the most intimate places of your heart if you let Him. Watch as He transforms you before your very eyes, and then share your stories of freedom with others. You never know what a blue sapphire ring, recycled hammock, or black bean brownies will do.

*Floating across the sand in my "wedding dress"
from Jesus just before sunset in Kona, Hawaii.*

ACKNOWLEDGMENTS

To my Best Friend and Lord of my life, who has weathered the greatest storms and congratulated me in conquering my deepest fears, thank You for continuing to reveal more of Your heart to me and for guiding me through the hard and the beautiful times. You are my everything, always.

To my friend and mentor, Jendayi, you have been a moral support, sounding board, and consistent prayer warrior in my life and throughout this birthing process. Thank you for who you are and for always believing in me.

To my "Jonathan" best friend on this earth, Sarah, thank you for choosing me through it all. Thank you for adventuring, praying, laughing, and crying with me. You make life possible because I know we will always have one another to hold each other's arms up in the battles (and to celebrate in the glories, too)!

To my creative friends, Taylor and Michaella, for your generosity and countless hours of prayer in seeking the heart of the Father with me throughout so much of my journey. Thank you for believing in me every step of the way, and for sewing into my steps of faith. Michaella, you are the master photo editor! Thank you!

To my brilliant designer and friend, Alison, you rock! Thanks for the giggles and smiles throughout our creative process. You did a fantastic job on the cover, and I cannot see what doors the Lord opens for your creativity!

To my wonderful editor and new friend, Edie, thank you for your insight and guidance. I couldn't have birthed this first book baby without your help. You are a joy and the missing piece I needed. I am thankful to have found myself in Hawaii with wonderful neighbors that brought us together.

To everyone who contributed to the blessings and memories in this book, thank you! God was working through you whether you knew it or not.

ABOUT THE AUTHOR

Megan is an adventurer, born and raised in south Denver where she received her business degree from the University of Colorado. She currently resides in Kona, Hawaii. She has a love for family, Kingdom business, fitness, dance, and her community of friends around the world. Megan has worked overseas and in several developing nations with a passion to eradicate sex trafficking and better the livelihoods of those living in poverty. In 2016, her heart for mental health and sustainable business led Megan to launch her fitness business. She is currently working on other programs to improve mental health in our world.

Made in the USA
Columbia, SC
22 October 2021